LIFE OR DEATH

Surviving the Impossible

Larry Verstraete

D0188514

Scholastic Canada Ltd.
Toronto New York London Auckland Sydney
Mexico City New Delhi Hong Kong Buenos Aires

For my granddaughter, Raeghan
— young, but already strong.
— L.V.

Scholastic Canada Ltd.
604 King Street West, Toronto, Ontario M5V 1E1, Canada

Scholastic Inc.
557 Broadway, New York, NY 10012, USA

Scholastic Australia Pty Limited
PO Box 579, Gosford, NSW 2250, Australia

Scholastic New Zealand Limited
Private Bag 94407, Botany, Manukau 2163, New Zealand

Scholastic Children's Books
Euston House, 24 Eversholt Street, London NW1 1DB, UK

www.scholastic.ca

Library and Archives Canada Cataloguing in Publication
Verstraete, Larry, author
Life or death : surviving the impossible / Larry Verstraete.
Issued in print and electronic formats.
ISBN 978-1-4431-1951-1 (pbk.).--ISBN 978-1-4431-3312-8 (html)
1. Survival--Juvenile literature. 2. Escapes--Juvenile literature.
I. Title.
G525.V375 2014   j613.6'9   C2013-905968-7
                          C2013-905969-5

6 5 4 3 2 1   Printed in Canada   121   14 15 16 17 18

TABLE OF CONTENTS

INTRODUCTION
Three life or death situations . . .

A teenager is trapped somewhere inside a city sewer system, breathing toxic air, fighting hypothermia and swimming against swirling water. No one knows his exact location, how to reach him, or even if he survived his roller-coaster ride through narrow pipes and fast-flowing waterways.

Minutes after takeoff a plane hits a flock of geese, destroying both engines and turning the aircraft into a dead weight. Airports are too far away to reach, and the plane is in a powerless glide, hurtling toward towering skyscrapers. The 155 people aboard brace for impact. In all likelihood, the death toll will be enormous.

Camp 14 is a brutal place where torture and abuse rule. One political prisoner — a scrawny young man — dreams of freedom. Freedom is on the other side of a heavily guarded, electrified fence that rings the camp. In the long history of Camp 14, no prisoner has ever escaped. Will this young man be the first?

In *Life or Death: Surviving the Impossible*, the stakes are high, the chances of survival remote and the path to a positive outcome riddled with pitfalls. In this book people come head-to-head with impossible situations. The odds are stacked against them. There is no light to point the way, and no map to follow that will lead them out. They must create their own.

Just what does it take to turn the tables, to beat impossible odds and triumph in the end? That is a question the stories in this book might answer.

LIFE OR DEATH – SURVIVE

ORDEAL ON MAMMOTH MOUNTAIN

Time was running out for snowboarder Eric Le Marque.

The moment he stepped off his snowboard, Eric Le Marque realized his mistake. The snow was waist-deep and in no time his gym socks and thin pants were soaked. The fierce wind whipped through his soggy clothes, sucking heat from his body. In the blizzard Le Marque couldn't see the distant ridge or the far-off trail that led down the mountain. "It was like I opened the door to another world," he said.

Over the past year, Le Marque, a former professional hockey player, had become a heavy drug user — a "puppet to my habit" as he put it. That morning he'd hit the slopes of California's Mammoth Mountain with his snowboard, craving excitement but hindered by the exhaustion, false sense of security and poor judgment that are a by-product of drug use.

3

Caught up in the thrill of snowboarding, Le Marque had ignored dark clouds rolling in from the east. Hoping for one last run before the storm hit, he'd set his sights on the ridge and the trail beyond. Midway there his snowboard had stalled, leaving him stranded just as the storm struck.

Le Marque was dressed in a light ski jacket and pants. He had taken along only a few belongings, things that now seemed pretty useless — like four pieces of bubble gum, a cell phone with a dying battery, an MP3 player, a twenty-dollar bill, the key to his condo and a baggie containing his daily dose of crystal meth. In his rush to leave, Le Marque hadn't let anyone know where he was going. Now he was lost and alone, enveloped in a blanket of snow, but convinced that if he kept moving he would find a way out.

Winds swirl around the heights of Mammoth Mountain.

Le Marque wandered for hours, shifting direction often. Using his snowboard as a shovel, he carved paths through ever-growing drifts. Sometimes, on downward slopes, he hopped rides on it. Then, well after midnight, Le Marque hunkered down for the night among blackened stumps in an area destroyed by a forest fire. Driven by hunger, he devoured the bubble gum in his pocket, the only food he had.

That long night was the first of many. By day Le Marque fought the cold, talked himself out of growing despair and tramped through snow. At night he found shelter in trenches or among trees. He hacked off bark and small branches with the sharp edge of his snowboard to make a mattress and ate whatever he could find — cedar bark, pine needles, seeds. When thirsty, he sucked on small quantities of snow. Sometimes he even drank his own urine. One day, frustrated and parched, he dumped out the crystal meth and used the empty baggie to melt snow. It was a critical moment — a first step toward overcoming his drug habit.

Occasionally there were glimmers of hope that he might survive. One day Le Marque found an empty beer can. He ripped off the top and bottom, then flattened out the middle. He tied the top and bottom pieces to his bindings to make shiny reflectors, believing they might signal would-be rescuers. The middle section of the can became a crude animal-alert device. Fastened to his jacket, it clanged as he walked, sending noisy warnings to wolves that lurked in the forest.

Sometimes Le Marque's flashes of creativity just spawned greater misery. Dehydrated, he searched for running water and found a fast-flowing river. Unable to reach the water because of deep snow, he remembered the twenty-dollar bill. He rolled the bill lengthwise, making it into a straw. Then he spread his body on a snow shelf above the river and stretched as far as he could to suck up cold water. Suddenly he heard a sharp *crack*. He felt the snow shift and his body slide. Before he could react, he was neck-deep in the icy river, being dragged by the swift current, his knees and shins bumping along the jagged bottom.

Eventually Le Marque pulled himself out, but the encounter left him bruised. The wind fanned his wet clothes, draining precious heat from his body. He lost feeling in his feet, and when he took off his waterlogged boots and socks, patches of frozen skin came with them.

His cell phone proved useless. There was no signal and the battery was nearly dead. Le Marque wandered, carving trails through the fresh snow, hoping that one would lead him out of the wilderness. Hunger pains were constant. He lost muscle mass, and his frame, once athletic and trim, took on a skeletal look. He plodded on feet black from frostbite and dead to all feeling. To keep moving, he set small goals. "I have to take at least ten steps," he told himself.

To boost his morale, Le Marque listened to his MP3 player. Then on the fourth day, he tried something new. Switching the MP3 player to FM mode, he turned the dial and locked on to a broadcast from a local radio station. The signal was weaker in some directions, stronger in others. That gave him an idea.

"By pointing the MP3 player at slightly different angles, I was able to get a bead on where the signal came in strongest," Le Marque wrote later. "That was the direction I headed in. I had come up with a crude sort of compass and could only hope that it would lead me to safety by the most direct route."

Over the next two days, Le Marque struggled up a steep slope, certain that there was a ski lodge somewhere on the other side. Hypothermia muddled his brain. He saw ghostly images in the forest, heard sounds that didn't exist and re-played nightmares that seemed all too real.

On the morning of the seventh day, Le Marque heard the drone of a distant plane. Desperately he tried to send a signal by turning on the MP3 player and pointing the tiny blue LED screen skyward, hoping that the pilot might see the faint glow. Instead the plane turned and disappeared, sending Le Marque into greater depths of despair.

He was dying. He knew it now. "For the rest of that day," he said, "I never left the shelter I had dug. The sun rose, clouds rolled overhead and the hours unwound as morning turned to midday and moved steadily on into the afternoon. It all passed me by. I may not have been dead yet, but it was hard to tell the difference."

Hypothermia muddled his brain. . . . He was dying.

On the morning of the eighth day, Le Marque had a remarkable moment of clarity. It was, as he put it, "as if a dense fog had lifted just before the onset of total darkness."

The battery on his MP3 player was almost dead, but Le Marque wondered what would happen if he turned the dial slightly, just enough to veer away from the radio station broadcast that he had captured earlier. Would that send a fuzzy signal, a beam of some kind or an electronic disruption, to alert those who might be searching for him?

Le Marque fumbled with the dial. The radio crackled and stuttered. Suddenly he heard his own name on a news report announcing that he was presumed dead and that a search for his body was underway.

Hope replaced despair. He wasn't dead. Not yet anyway, and to hear that searchers were looking for him was encouraging. He vowed to stay alive, to hang on just a bit longer.

Shortly after, Le Marque heard the sound of a helicopter. He struggled to his feet, searched the horizon through eyes blinded by the sun and spotted a blurry object in the sky. As it approached, he waved frantically. The helicopter hovered over him, whipping clouds of snow with its blades. A door opened. A figure in a silver suit slid down a rope.

"Are you Eric Le Marque?" the man asked.

Patrollers on snowmobiles searching for Le Marque had discovered a snowboard trail heading south. They'd passed on the information to the National Guard, who'd sent a Black Hawk chopper to scour the back side of the mountain. Using infrared imaging, they had detected a heat source — Le Marque, still alive, staggering through the snow.

Although Eric Le Marque's ordeal on Mammoth Mountain was over, the road to recovery was just beginning. His body temperature had dropped to 30° Celsius, 7° below normal. He was hypothermic and dehydrated. In eight days he had lost 18 kilograms, about 20 per cent of his usual weight. Worst of all, his feet were severely frostbitten. Pus oozed from cracks and blisters. The skin was mottled, black as charred wood in places, vivid red in others. The dead feeling had advanced, too, creeping beyond his feet and farther up his legs.

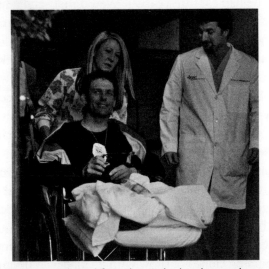

Le Marque emerged from his ordeal a changed person, and went on to become an inspirational speaker.

Eric Le Marque spent months in hospital undergoing rounds of surgery. To save his life, doctors amputated his legs below the knees and fitted him with prosthetic limbs. With typical determination, Eric fought through depression and painful therapy, adjusting to his new legs, overcoming his dependency on drugs and creating a new life for himself.

TWENTY-TWO YEARS IN A TOMB

To stay alive, Juad Amir Sayed had to convince others that he was already dead.

On December 2, 1981, twenty-four-year-old Juad Amir Sayed disappeared. His neighbours in Karada, Iraq, never saw him leave the house. Even his closest cousins didn't know his whereabouts. Sayed was there one day, gone the next.

During the regime of Iraqi president Saddam Hussein, citizens often disappeared. Saddam's secret police combed the country, hunting those suspected of being threats to the dictator. Arrests were common. Arrest led to prison, sometimes torture, and often swift execution without so much as a trial. Sometimes those arrested simply vanished, never to be heard from again.

Juad Sayed was one of the hunted, a man marked for arrest by the secret police. A young soldier, he had deserted the Iraqi army during the Iran-Iraq War, an act of treason punishable by death. On top of that, Sayed was a follower of the banned Dawa Party, a Shiite Muslim group that had opposed Saddam for decades. Then there was a foiled escape attempt. Desperate to leave

9

Iraq, Sayed had planned to flee to Iran with a cousin. The secret police discovered the plan. His cousin was arrested and hanged. Sayed feared he would be next. It was just a matter of time.

When Sayed went missing that December day, his neighbours and relatives assumed that the secret police had captured him. They assumed he was either dead already or languishing in some far-off prison, another victim of Saddam's madness. And that is exactly what Sayed wanted them to think.

"I was trapped in Karada and there was nothing else I could do," he said.

It took him a week to enact his plan. With the help of his mother, Aziza Masak Dahish, Sayed packed his Dawa books into a flour sack and buried them in the ground. To eliminate all traces of his existence, he burned his identity card. He dug a tunnel that led to a concrete room he had built below the family kitchen. The room was small — just 1 metre wide by 1.5 metres long. A vent up to the roof of the house brought in fresh air; a tiny peephole let in a ray of sunshine.

Juad Amir Sayed began a life of self-imposed exile.

Sayed equipped the tiny space with a few necessities — a small hot plate to heat food, a battery-operated radio with headphones to keep track of the news, a bare light bulb wired to the wall for times when there was electricity, a kerosene lamp for times when there wasn't. He installed a small toilet and added other features: a clock, shelves to hold books, hooks to hold a mirror, a toothbrush and other essentials.

Feet first, Sayed squeezed his bony frame through a small square hole in the kitchen floor. His mother slid a concrete lid over the opening, covered it with a flattened cardboard box and pushed an empty bed over top. And with that, he began a life of self-imposed exile.

Only Sayed's mother and his four siblings knew of his underground existence and they were sworn to secrecy. While the family lived a normal life above, Sayed lived below, squirrelled away in the tiny chamber, protected from Saddam and his mob.

Day after day Sayed followed a similar routine. He prepared simple meals of beans and rice with supplies his mother passed to him through the hole in the kitchen floor. He washed his frayed robe in water drawn from a pipe hammered into the ground which served as a well. To pass the time, he practised calligraphy and spent hours reading prayers from the Koran, the Muslim holy book. At night he slept on the hard-packed dirt, his body curled to fit in the small space.

Life below was often lonely. "Most of the time, it was very, very quiet," Sayed said. "I think only death could be so quiet."

A tiny peephole, barely the width of a finger, became Sayed's window on the world. When his brother got married in the courtyard, Sayed watched through the peephole, rejoicing from a safe distance. Through it Sayed studied nature, finding happiness in small changes — the wind bending branches of nearby trees, the sky turning pink at sunset, water spilling off the roof after a rainfall. Each moment was a golden promise that life would be better someday.

As years passed, the view through the peephole became smaller. A date palm outside grew tall and spread its branches over the opening. In time it blocked the peephole completely, eliminating the source of Sayed's simple pleasure. Still he hung on to hope, counting down the days to freedom.

There were a few close calls. Once, while the family was

asleep, a policeman entered the house. Sayed's mother found the man searching the kitchen, dangerously close to the bed that covered the opening. She screamed. A neighbour rushed over firing a shotgun and the intruder ran, never to return. Sayed's location remained a secret.

Sayed's mother came to his rescue another time, too. While building a cesspool in his yard, a neighbour used a backhoe. The machine chewed the earth, coming close to Sayed's underground cell. Fearing that the wall might collapse and bury Sayed, his mother ran out and threw herself in front of the machine. Construction stopped and her son was saved.

Another time, while visiting Sayed's family, a thirteen-year-old cousin rolled under the bed in the kitchen. He discovered the lid, opened it and came face to face with Sayed, a man who was supposed to be dead. In shock, the boy ran home. "A ghost! I've seen a ghost!" he told his mother. Guessing that it was Sayed, the boy's mother swore her son to silence and mentioned it to no one.

To keep abreast of the news, Sayed listened to his radio. As the years clicked past, he tracked major events: the dismantling of the Berlin Wall in 1989; the Iraqi invasion of Kuwait in 1990; the election of George W. Bush as president of the United States in 2000. In the fall of 2001, shortly after the terrorist attacks on the United States, Sayed heard George Bush speak, promising that the terrorists would be hunted down.

Then in early 2003, Sayed heard another announcement. The US and a coalition of other countries were beginning a new campaign. Claiming that Saddam had been instrumental in the terrorist assaults of 9/11, and that he might be harbouring nuclear weapons, coalition forces were launching an attack on Iraq.

A statue of dictator Saddam Hussein is pulled down
in Baghdad in April 2003.

For Sayed, this was good news. The dictator was a marked
man, his days of oppression were numbered . . . and so were
Sayed's days of confinement in the cramped space below the
family kitchen.

Sayed's home was near an air base and ammunition
depot, and from his secret place he heard sounds of hope
— the scream of coalition aircraft as they raked the base,
the *rat-tat-tat* of artillery fire, the thunder of bombs as they
detonated.

Then on April 9, 2003, three weeks into the campaign,
Sayed's radio crackled with exciting news. Coalition forces
had been successful. Saddam was on the run. Iraq was free
of the dictator.

As a safeguard, Sayed waited one more day. When he heard
that US troops had pulled down a statue of Saddam in Baghdad, he felt it was finally safe. Almost twenty-two years after
going into hiding, and now forty-six years old, Sayed emerged.

His neighbours were shocked. The man they had thought

was dead or missing was alive, but barely recognizable. After being in his cramped, dark quarters for so long, Sayed's back was stooped, his legs were wobbly and his eyes were no longer used to bright sunlight. He had difficulty walking and had to wear sunglasses. Due to a lack of calcium in his diet, many of his teeth had fallen out, too.

Adjustment to life above ground was not easy for Sayed. Sometimes when he needed comfort afterwards, he would return to his familiar tomb to curl up on the dirt floor that had been his mattress for so long. "It is my second home," Sayed explained. "Maybe it is my first. I will leave it like it is."

SURVIVING THE IMPOSSIBLE
January 12, 2010 / Port au Prince, Haiti

When Hotel Montana collapsed during an earthquake that devastated much of Haiti, American journalist Dan Woolley lay trapped in a hollow pocket under six storeys of fallen concrete. The back of his head throbbed, a sign of a possible concussion, and when Woolley reached to check it, he got a handful of blood. Searing pain shot up his leg, too, indicating a possible fracture. Weak from his injuries, Woolley worried that at any moment aftershocks might pancake the building, completely burying him under rubble before help arrived.

Woolley tried to find a safer spot, but in the dark he couldn't see anything. Then he felt a bump against his chest from something dangling around his neck. It was the digital camera that he had forgotten he was carrying. Woolley aimed the camera into the dark, pressed the shutter and took multiple shots around him. He viewed the results on the screen. Each shot told him something about his position, the obstacles around him, the routes leading away.

One picture showed an elevator shaft with a small elevator car wedged inside, its door frozen open. Surrounded by thick walls, the elevator car offered protection and safety in case of further collapse. Woolley dragged himself to it, carefully steering around rubble and electrical cables. He crammed his tall frame into the tight space.

Using the flash on the camera, Woolley examined his injuries. His leg was worse than he imagined. A ragged gash ran from his knee to his ankle. Blood trickled from the wound. Given the rate of blood loss and the possibility of infection, he worried he'd never make it until rescuers arrived.

Huddled in the dark, Woolley waited and prayed. He thought about his family, his wife and young children. Then he remembered his cell phone.

Digging it out of his pocket, Woolley switched it on. Although he wasn't able to secure a connection, he located a first-aid app he had downloaded earlier. By following directions on the app, he treated his wounds using materials around him — peeling off his sock to make a compress for the back of his head, tearing off his shirt to fashion a bandage for his leg. To tie the shirt, he found a wire in the elevator and ripped it from the wall.

The app warned about the dangers of shock, a

life-threatening condition that often accompanies severe injury. *Stay awake*, the app suggested. *If you feel yourself slipping into shock, do not succumb to sleep.* As a safeguard, Woolley set the cell phone's alarm clock to rouse him every twenty minutes.

"It really was an incredible tool in my pocket," he said of the cell phone, "and I was really glad to have it."

After sixty-five hours, rescuers found Dan Woolley and pulled him from the wreckage, dehydrated and badly injured, but grateful for the technology that had given him a second chance at life.

COMPLETELY ALONE

Hurled from the plane, Juliane Koepcke saw the jungle whirling toward her.

To this day, Juliane Koepcke remembers the exact moment the plane exploded. It was around 1:30 p.m. on Christmas Eve, 1971. She was seventeen years old, one of 92 passengers aboard a turboprop L-188 Electra. Juliane was sitting beside her mother in a row of three seats near the back. They were flying to Pucallpa, Peru, to join her father, who ran a wildlife research station there.

Thirty minutes into the one-hour flight, the plane entered a pitch-black cloud. Lightning flashed. The plane shook. Luggage fell out of overhead compartments. For ten terrifying minutes, the plane bucked the storm. And then Juliane saw a blinding white light along the right wing . . . heard her mother saying, "Now it's all over" . . . people screaming . . . engines roaring . . . Seconds later she heard nothing but the sound of wind whistling in her ears.

Suddenly Juliane was outside the plane, still strapped to her seat, flying upside down in a free fall. She wasn't scared, just numb. She felt the seat belt pressing into her stomach. She saw the Amazon jungle — like "green cauliflower" — rushing toward her. Then she blacked out.

When Juliane woke up, it was morning. She was lying under her seat in the jungle. She wasn't strapped in any longer, and it was raining. She had no memory of the impact or what followed — just hazy recollections of the whirling plunge. Somehow she must have woken up earlier though, she realized, and released her seat belt to crawl under the seat, probably to get out of the rain.

Gone was her mother who had been sitting beside her. Gone, too, was the heavy-set man who had occupied the third seat near the aisle. There was no sign of anyone else. No bodies, no wreckage from the plane, just dense foliage all around.

Juliane's head ached. So did her shoulder. Her right eye was swollen and gashes ran along her arms and legs. Later Juliane would find out that she had broken her collarbone and suffered a concussion, but in the jungle that day she felt little pain, just confusion. As her thoughts cleared, truth hit home. Through some miracle, she had survived a 3000-metre free fall. Now she was alone.

Juliane tried to walk but, overcome by dizziness, she blacked out. For much of that day and night she drifted in and out of consciousness. Finally she felt strong enough to crawl.

She had no idea where she was. Other than a small bag of candy found among bits of debris on the ground, she had no food or supplies. She had lost her glasses and one of her sandals, and she was wearing only a short, sleeveless mini-dress.

In a daze, she searched for wreckage, for some sign of life. "Hello. Is anyone there?" she called over and over.

The dense canopy of the Amazon rainforest was going to make searching for survivors nearly impossible.

On the afternoon of the second day, Juliane heard a promising sound — water bubbling somewhere. She followed the sound to a small stream. Immediately she recognized its potential. Both of her parents were zoologists. Having lived with them at research stations, Juliane had learned a few survival skills. Water, her father had taught her, always flowed downhill toward larger bodies of water. Follow the flow of a stream and it will eventually join a river. Somewhere along the river you will find a village, a town or some other human settlement.

Juliane heeded her father's words. She had a destination now, and there was no point in staying where she was, alone and surrounded by jungle. She followed the stream, picking her way through thick stands of trees, heading on a course she hoped would take her to the research station.

Several times a day it rained. When the sun finally broke through the canopy, the jungle turned into a steamy cauldron. Heat and humidity sapped Juliane's strength. At night she rested on the bank. When temperatures dropped, she shivered in her thin dress and curled up to conserve warmth. Drawn to the scent of her perspiration and blood, squadrons of mosquitoes attacked. Gnats crawled into her ears. Her sleep was broken by nightmares.

On the fourth day Juliane heard the distinctive splash of a king vulture landing on the water. She knew that vultures fed off corpses. The sound filled her with dread. There were bodies from the plane crash nearby. She was sure of it. Would one of them be her mother?

As she rounded a bend in the stream, Juliane spotted a row of airplane seats jammed upside down in the mud. Three bodies were strapped in the seats. The impact had buried the upper parts a half-metre into the ground, exposing only the legs and feet. One of the bodies looked like a woman's.

Juliane had never seen a dead body before. Paralyzed by fear, but driven by a need to know, she pried off one of the shoes with a stick. The toenails were painted with nail polish, something her mother never did. Juliane felt relief and then a moment later, shame. How could she be so stupid? The body couldn't possibly be her mother's. Her mother had been strapped in the seat beside her.

With every new step, Juliane thought about her parents. Was her mother injured, lying in pain somewhere and needing help? And her father? He must have heard the news. How was he coping, alone now, with both his wife and daughter missing?

Occasionally Juliane heard the buzz of search planes. She yelled and waved, trying to get their attention, but the thick canopy obscured the view. Unable to see her, the planes drifted farther away. In time, the buzzing stopped completely. More than ever she felt alone. *They've given up on me!* she thought.

Juliane slogged on, fighting exhaustion and despair. Her clothes were caked in mud; her skin was burnt from the sun;

the bag of candy was long gone. She didn't have a knife or cooking equipment, and she knew that much of what grew in the jungle was poisonous. She didn't dare eat.

One day she heard an encouraging sound — the call of a hoatzin, a native bird. She knew from her experience at the research station that hoatzins lived only near large, open rivers. Juliane followed the bird call, winding through thickets until she came to a wide river. Driven by the promise of a settlement downstream, she followed it.

Juliane knew not to walk along the banks, places where deadly snakes crawled and poisonous spiders hid. Instead she waded in the middle of the river, away from the shallows that piranhas preferred. Now and then she saw wildlife along the banks — howler monkeys, martens, brocket deer. The animals displayed no fear, none of the usual caution that animals familiar with people show. Perhaps there was no settlement nearby after all.

Juliane pushed doubt aside. "I wasn't in pain or panic, but I knew that I had to rely on my own strength to get out of there."

A new problem arose. She had a small open sore on her upper right arm. Flies had laid eggs inside. The eggs had hatched, and now tiny white maggots squirmed underneath her skin, feeding off her flesh and carving a tunnel for themselves. Juliane squeezed her skin to push out the maggots, but the hole was too deep. She bent her ring into a hook and tried fishing them out. That didn't work either. Neither did flicking them out with a stick.

By the afternoon of the tenth day, Juliane was too weak to continue. Wrapped in loneliness and misery, she rested on the riverbank. She slept in the sun, her back against a tree for protection in case a creature approached from behind. Her mind reeled with dreams of rescue.

When Juliane woke up, she spotted something she hadn't noticed earlier — a wooden boat. She inched over and touched it to prove to herself that it was real. Near the boat, Juliane found a little path that led up a hill into the jungle. It was hard to crawl up the hill — it seemed to take ages — but at the top, Juliane discovered a small hut. It had no walls, just poles that supported a palm-leaf roof.

"I had to rely on my own strength to get out of there."

In the hut, Juliane found a boat motor and a barrel of diesel fuel covered with a plastic tarp. Her open wound was worse than before. The maggots wriggled, digging deeper, and Juliane worried that her arm might have to be amputated. She remembered that her family once had a dog with a similar problem. Her father had doused the dog's wound with kerosene to flush out the maggots. Would it work for her?

She found a plastic tube in the hut. She sucked up diesel fuel from the barrel, sprinkled some on the open sore and rode through the pain. The maggots squirmed, trying to escape. Quickly Juliane plucked about thirty maggots from the wound before the rest tunnelled deeper and disappeared.

That night and the next morning, Juliane slept in the hut. She huddled beneath the tarp, listening to the patter of rain, too weak and discouraged to care if she lived or died. When the rain stopped in the afternoon, her dark mood lifted. There had to be people nearby, she realized. The hut and boat were proof of that. Hope renewed, she decided to spend another night in the hut and make a fresh start in the morning.

At the same moment she made her decision, Juliane heard voices — men talking in Spanish. "It was like hearing the sound of angels," she said.

Three men emerged from the jungle. They stared in disbelief at her, unsure if she was real or some forest phantom. Juliane told her story. There was a plane crash . . . somehow she survived . . . she was trying to find her father . . .

The men treated her wounds and gave her food. The next morning they took her by boat to a town along the river. Medics at the local hospital treated her injuries and pulled more than 50 maggots from the small hole in her arm. After a brief stay, she was reunited with her father. It was a joyous moment, but one tinged with sadness. Juliane was alive, but her mother? Despite the odds, her father held out hope that perhaps his wife, too, had survived.

With directions provided by Juliane, a search party zeroed in on the crash area. They found the plane, the mangled parts and scattered luggage and the bodies spread over a wide area. On January 12 they identified Juliane's mother — dead like all the others.

"Then it was real," Juliane said.

Survivor Juliane Koepcke, right, writes a note to friends after recovering from injuries received in a Christmas Eve plane crash.

News of Juliane's miraculous survival spread around the globe. She was hounded for interviews and received letters from complete strangers. Suddenly famous, she craved a normal life. For almost three decades she declined interviews and kept her memories suppressed. Then in 1999 at the request of filmmaker Werner Herzog, who wanted to make a documentary about her, Juliane returned to the crash site. It was time, she decided.

Although the jungle had grown thicker, little else had changed. The plane wreck was still there, hidden in the tangled undergrowth. Prodded by Herzog's questions, Juliane relived the past. It was a healing experience. Dealing with haunting memories and long-buried emotions was, in her words, "the best therapy."

⚠ FACING THE IMPOSSIBLE
January 17, 2011 / Rakkestad, Norway

Thirteen-year-old Walter Eikrem was walking home from the bus stop like every other day when he spotted something grey on the snowy hillside. "At first, I thought it might have been the neighbour's dogs," he said.

The grey shapes turned out to be four wolves. Not uncommon in the area of Norway where Walter lived, wolves had been spotted just the day before. Walter recalled his mother's advice: *Don't run away. That just invites the wolves to hunt you down.*

"But I was so afraid that I couldn't even run away if I wanted to," Walter said.

Fearing that the wolves might attack, he stood his ground. Calmly he pulled out the earbuds he was wearing, unhooked them from his cell phone and cranked up the volume. Aiming the phone at the wolves, he waved his arms, screamed at the top of his lungs and blasted a hard-rock song at them.

"They didn't really get scared," Walter said. "They just turned around and simply walked away."

CONFRONTING THE IMPOSSIBLE
September 8, 2013 / Churchill, Manitoba

Late at night, as Garett Kolsun walked along a deserted street of this northern Canadian town, he spotted a polar bear approaching from behind. "It was running full tilt towards me," he said.

Alone and with no place to hide, Kolsun screamed for help. He ran in circles, dodging blows and bites, all the while yelling frantically. To defend himself, he flailed his arms and shoved back. Finally he fled to a bakery and tried kicking down the door.

"At that point, the bear was basically on top of me," he said.

Kolsun pulled his cell phone out and thrust the lighted screen into the bear's face. Startled, the bear stepped back, knocked over a planter, swung its head to look behind and gave Kolsun the break he badly needed. He ran to a house and took refuge inside. Apart from a few scratches to his chest and two puncture wounds on his hip, Kolsun was safe and unharmed.

A RIBBON OF GREY

With 155 people aboard his disabled plane, the pilot needed a place to land.

One minute after takeoff from New York's LaGuardia Airport on January 15, 2009, co-pilot Jeffrey Skiles spotted a flock of geese. A moment later so did the pilot, Chesley "Sully" Sullenberger, a veteran with forty years of flying experience. The birds were dead ahead, dark dots against the blue sky, and about the length of a football field away.

The twin-engine US Airways Airbus A320 was steadily climbing, the streets of Manhattan were fading away and the geese were too close to avoid. The plane ripped through the formation, sucking several birds into both engines. Caught in a giant blender of whirling blades, flesh, bone and feathers mashed into "bird slurry."

Several loud bangs sounded. Inside the engines, impellers broke. Vanes blew apart, guides fractured and both engines quit. Blood splattered the windshield. The smell of burnt flesh drifted into the cockpit as lights on the console flashed and alarms signalled danger.

In the cabin behind, 3 flight attendants and 150 passengers

felt a jolt. Through the windows they saw flames shooting from the engines. Smoke rolled through the cabin, carrying the stench of jet fuel. Instead of the normal engine drone, there was sudden silence. One flight attendant said it was like being in a library.

In the cockpit, pilot and co-pilot ran through a carefully practised routine. "My aircraft," Sullenberger said to Skiles. In those two words, the men established protocols. Each knew what the other would do. Sullenberger would operate the controls. Skiles would run through the emergency checklist and try to restart the engines.

The emergency checklist was a three-page catalogue of steps to follow. Within thirty seconds, Skiles was at the end of the list. The engines wouldn't start. It was unlikely they ever would. The plane was a 70-tonne dead weight gliding without power over Manhattan, one of the world's most densely populated cities.

Sullenberger radioed air traffic control. "Hit birds. We've lost thrust on both engines. We're turning back toward LaGuardia." His voice sounded calm in spite of the emergency.

Air traffic control checked runways, looking for clearance at LaGuardia Airport for an emergency landing. In the seconds that elapsed, Sullenberger realized a few facts. The plane was quickly losing altitude, dropping at a rate of 300 metres per minute. LaGuardia was too far away. They'd never make it.

"Could we land at Teterboro Airport instead?" he asked air traffic control. Teterboro was closer than LaGuardia, just across the Hudson River that separated Manhattan from New Jersey. Their chances would be better there.

Controllers called Teterboro. In moments they radioed Sullenberger with an answer. Teterboro it was. They had clearance, a runway set aside for the crippled plane.

By then the plane was flying lower, skimming above the skyline of Manhattan. Without engines, it was locked in a powerless glide. There was a good chance the plane would never make Teterboro, Sullenberger figured. It might slam into Manhattan instead. The death toll would be enormous.

Sullenberger would need all his skills to avoid hitting the densely crowded buildings of Manhattan.

In a double-engine failure when airports are too far away, the pilot normally looks for smooth pavement to bring down the plane — a major road, an empty highway. But Manhattan was crammed with buildings. There were no open spaces. Except one — the Hudson River, a wide ribbon of unruffled grey water.

"We're gonna be in the Hudson," Sullenberger announced. There was confidence in his voice. Sullenberger knew the plane. He knew the river, too. He was sure he could land the plane safely there.

Sullenberger wheeled the plane into a series of tight left turns to line it up with the river. "Brace for impact," he told passengers.

In the cabin, flight attendants gave directions. "Heads down! Stay down! Brace, brace!"

It was hard not to panic. "Everyone started, to be honest, to say prayers," one of the passengers reported. There was a rush of last-minute preparations. Martin and Tess Sosa hugged their two children. One was nine-month-old Damian, the youngest passenger on the plane. Vallie Collins texted her husband: *My plane is crashing.* She hoped it wouldn't be her last message. Eric Stevenson took out a business card and wrote a note to his mother and sister: *Mom and Jane, I love you.* He tucked the card into his front pocket. If he didn't make it, he hoped someone would find the card and get the message to his family.

Ferries and boats patrolled the river, but there were broad, open patches clear of vessels, too. Sullenberger aimed for the middle of the North River section of the Hudson. It was clear of obstacles, but near three boat terminals that might come to their rescue.

Operating the elevators and rudders, Sullenberger guided the plane. The aircraft had to be perfectly level when it landed. Too sharp a turn or too wide an angle and a wing tip might strike the water first, cartwheeling the fuselage, disintegrating the plane and spewing debris across the Hudson.

Belly flat, wings perfectly level and travelling at 240 kilometres per hour, the plane sliced the river, carving a deep wake as it slid to a stop.

"That wasn't as bad as I thought," Sullenberger and Skiles said to each other at the same time.

The impact jolted passengers, yanking them forward. "Coming down was like a roller-coaster ride," one said.

The impact ripped holes in the fuselage. The cargo doors popped open. Immediately water seeped into the cabin from the rear of the plane. Caught in the river's current, the downed plane floated south.

While Skiles ran through the evacuation checklist, Sullenberger opened the cockpit door. "Evacuate," he ordered.

Flight attendants took charge, opening the two front doors and directing passengers to do the same with the mid-cabin emergency exits. With the plane submerged up to its windows, people clambered over seats, rushing to the front as they tried to escape.

"It was controlled chaos," passenger Dave Sanderson said. "We had survived the crash, but we were going to drown."

Once outside, some passengers leaped into the water. Others stood on inflatable sliders, knee-deep in the icy river. Most, though, gathered on the wings with the frigid water lapping at their feet.

Passengers balance along the wings of the downed plane.

Sullenberger, Skiles and a few passengers gathered life vests, jackets, coats and blankets to hand to people on the wings. The temperature outside was minus 6° Celsius, but the wind made it seem colder. The wing was slick — "Like an ice rink," one passenger said.

Twice Sullenberger calmly walked the aisle, making sure that no one was still inside. Then he joined the others on the wing, the last one to vacate the cabin.

Within minutes a ferry pulled alongside the plane. Shortly after, vessels from the New York City Fire and Police Departments arrived. Still in charge, Sullenberger directed rescuers, advising them to take passengers off the wings first, since they were in greater danger than those on the inflatable sliders. Many were soggy and shivering. To ward off the cold, some of the rescue crew gave their jackets to freezing passengers.

All 155 passengers and crew survived. David Paterson, the governor of New York, said, "I believe that today we have had a miracle on the Hudson."

Sullenberger was hailed as a hero, a man with steely nerves and quick-thinking determination. He downplayed the attention, giving credit to his years of flying experience instead. In his book, *Highest Duty*, Sullenberger wrote: "I did not think I was going to die. Based on my experience, I was confident that I could make an emergency water landing that was survivable. That confidence was stronger than any fear."

OUTSMARTING THE IMPOSSIBLE
November 5, 2005 / Near Somalia, Africa

Passengers and crew of the cruise ship *Seabourn Spirit* awoke to the sound of gunfire and rocket-propelled grenades being fired across the bow. Pirates in two powerboats were speeding toward the ship, aiming to board the vessel, rob passengers and take hostages for ransom.

Quickly changing course, the captain, Sven Erik Pedersen, steered the *Seabourn Spirit* into open water to evade the attackers. When the pirates followed, Pedersen tried to ram their boats and swamp them with waves from the ship's wake. In the meantime

Michael Groves, the *Seabourn Spirit*'s security officer, unwound a high-pressure hose and blasted the pirates with a powerful jet of water.

When the pirates continued the attack, Som Bahadur Gruing, the master at arms, scrambled to unleash the *Seabourn Spirit*'s secret weapon. Called a Long Range Acoustic Device (LRAD), the device was about the size and shape of a TV satellite dish. When aimed at a target and activated, the LRAD emitted a deafening shrill, capable of causing permanent damage to hearing from a distance of more than 300 metres.

The LRAD had been used by US troops in Iraq to disorient and confuse the enemy. It had been used to control crowds in New Orleans after Hurricane Katrina. With pirate attacks growing more frequent along the coast of Somalia, it had been rigged to the vessel as an experimental safeguard. It had never been tested on a ship zigzagging through open waters and never used against pirates with a history of bloody encounters. Would it work now?

As Gruing tried to activate the LRAD, he was struck by a bullet to his upper body.

Groves was nearby. "I saw a spray of blood and he just went straight down. I thought he was gone, but he opened one eye."

Quickly, Groves dragged the injured man away. After securing him in a safe place, Groves returned to the LRAD. He trained it on the pirates and opened fire, blasting a tight beam of sound at the moving targets.

At first the pirates resisted. They skirted around the ship, firing machine guns and grenades, looking for gaps in the liner's defences. But after thirty minutes of ear-splitting screeching, they gave up. As the pirates retreated, the *Seabourn Spirit* escaped to deeper waters, putting distance between itself and the attackers.

LIFE OR DEATH – RESCUE

AN EPIDEMIC OF FEAR

Typhus was a deadly disease, but exactly the tool the doctor needed.

A dry cough wracked the young Polish man's body. His forehead was hot to the touch, and his clothes were drenched with sweat. The man complained of headaches, muscle pain, constant tiredness and teeth-chattering chills that never seemed to go away.

His doctor, Eugene Lazowski, recognized the symptoms. The patient had the flu. The flu rarely killed and, given proper treatment — fluids to drink, lots of bedrest, perhaps some aspirin — the doctor knew the man would recover.

From his medical bag, Dr. Lazowski retrieved a small vial containing a liquid. He drew a sample with a syringe and swabbed the young man's arm. Just a pinprick of pain, that's all you'll feel, he reassured the man. Then, just as he had with dozens of patients before, Dr. Lazowski injected the liquid into the man's body.

The law required that the doctor submit a sample of the

man's blood. He knew what would happen then, the panic it would create among the Nazis, the chaos that would follow. In German-occupied Poland during World War II, fear governed every move. The patient would survive, no worse for the injection, but the Germans would act quickly.

It was exactly what the doctor wanted. One injection at a time, one blood test after another, he was saving thousands of lives by fighting a very different kind of war.

* * *

In occupied Poland, helping Jews was a crime punishable by death. Dr. Lazowski's own parents had hidden Jewish families in their home, and he felt he could — and should — do something, too. "My profession is to save lives and prevent death. I was fighting for life," he explained.

German soldiers march into Warsaw, Poland, in early October 1939, shortly after the city was captured.

He started with small but daring acts of disobedience. From his house in Rozwadow, Poland, the doctor could see the wire fence that separated his yard from the Jewish ghetto behind it. The ghetto was a heavily guarded section of the city where Jews were corralled and held like prisoners, their rights and freedoms denied. In the cramped, filthy living conditions, bacteria thrived, disease spread quickly and deaths were frequent. To the Nazis, who were intent on eliminating Jews, an outbreak of disease in a ghetto was a bonus. No medical aid was provided. No doctors were permitted to help, and those who did faced the stiffest of penalties.

Dr. Lazowski arranged a secret signal. A white cloth tied to the fence meant that someone inside the ghetto was ill. Under the cover of darkness, he then smuggled medication and bandages into the ghetto, offered medical advice and tended to the sick. To throw the Germans off his trail, the doctor fudged official reports and exaggerated the quantities of medical supplies he used for his non-Jewish patients.

His was a small-scale operation, one pain soothed at a time, one Jewish life saved every so often. It might have continued this way, but then a chance discovery changed everything.

Of all the diseases common during the war, typhus was the one most feared by the Nazis. Many of the initial symptoms of typhus were similar to the flu — muscle pain, headache, exhaustion, chills. But with typhus, things quickly worsened. Patients with typhus developed a pink rash that turned bright red as it spread over the body. They developed high fevers and hacking coughs, and became delirious and dehydrated. And while many people recovered from the flu, typhus was often fatal. Untreated, it spread quickly, becoming a deadly epidemic.

To the German occupiers, an outbreak of typhus inside a ghetto was viewed as a blessing. Outside the ghetto, though, such an outbreak was a huge problem. The disease wiped out entire regiments, leaving the Nazis weak and defenceless. Typhus also took the lives of healthy, young Poles, reducing the number of slave labourers available to work at German farms and factories and putting a huge dent in the Nazi war effort.

Doctors who suspected that a patient had typhus were required by law to submit blood samples to German-controlled laboratories for testing. There the blood was mixed with a killed strain of bacteria known as Proteus OX19. If the patient had typhus, the sample clumped and turned cloudy.

While running tests, Dr. Stanislaw Matulewicz, a fellow physician, made a curious discovery. Healthy patients injected with dead Proteus OX19 bacteria didn't get sick with typhus, but their blood samples showed the same cloudy results. To those who didn't know any better, it would seem that the patient had typhus when, in fact, the patient was typhus-free.

When Dr. Lazowski learned of this discovery, he quickly spotted an opportunity to save even more lives. Together the two men launched a perilous but clever scheme.

Whenever they encountered a gentile patient who was suffering from the flu or who had symptoms remotely resembling typhus, they injected dead Proteus OX19 bacteria into that patient's bloodstream. As required by law, they drew blood samples and sent them to German-approved labs. Predictably, the patients tested positive for typhus. Just as predictably, this sent German officials into a frenzy.

Signs were posted around infected areas: *Achtung, Fleckfieber* — *Warning Typhus*. The areas were quarantined to restrict movement. The deportation of workers was stopped. German troops kept their distance, avoiding neighbouring ghettos and halting their relentless killing of Jews in the area.

Working this way, the two doctors created false epidemics

in a number of Polish villages. To protect themselves, they referred some of their injected patients to other doctors who were not in on the plot. Working independently, these doctors "discovered" typhus, too.

To the Germans, Dr. Lazowski seemed brave — working with those most infected, willing to risk his own life to save theirs. In private, though, he felt far from courageous. "I was scared, of course. I didn't know if I would be arrested and tortured by the Gestapo [German secret police]."

A German soldier guards a group of Polish men.

Despite the cover-up, by late 1943 German officials became suspicious. Typhus had been diagnosed a number of times, yet strangely no one seemed to be dying. An investigation was

37

launched, and a team of soldiers and doctors was dispatched to one of the quarantined areas.

When Dr. Lazowski heard about the approaching investigation, he gathered the oldest, sickest, most frail-looking patients he could find. All of them showed symptoms of typhus, though none had the disease. He injected them with Proteus OX19 and then housed them in the filthiest quarters he could find.

Dr. Lazowski met the visiting inspectors just outside the city. He welcomed them warmly and led them inside, where he served a hot meal. He filled glasses with vodka and passed them around the table. Then he soothed the inspectors with music and song. It was hard for anyone to leave, which is exactly what he hoped would happen.

"They were having such a good time they sent the younger doctors to make the examination," Dr. Lazowski said. "I told them to be my guest and examine the patients, but to be careful because the Polish are dirty and full of lice, which transfer typhus."

Plied with liquor and song, and stoked with false fears, the inexperienced doctors visited the sick. Worried for their own safety, they rushed through the examinations, drawing blood samples from only a few before leaving in a hurry. As planned, the samples tested positive for typhus and the inspection team cleared Dr. Lazowski of any wrongdoing.

Still, the Germans watched him closely. Toward the end of the war, a young German soldier who had once been treated by the doctor pulled his motorcycle up to Dr. Lazowski's office.

"Doctor, run, you are on the Gestapo hit list," the soldier told him.

Dr. Lazowski heeded the warning. Taking his wife and young daughter, he fled.

Working the typhus scheme, Doctors Eugene Lazowski and Stanislaw Matulewicz created fake epidemics in twelve villages during the war and rescued an estimated eight thousand men, women and children, Jews and non-Jews alike.

"I was not able to fight with a gun or a sword, but I found a way to scare the Germans," Dr. Lazowski said.

"HOUSTON, WE'VE HAD A PROBLEM HERE"

Three astronauts were stranded in space, marooned between Earth and the moon.

On April 13, 1970, astronaut Jack Swigert flipped a switch on the control panel of Apollo 13's command module. It was a routine act, one that had been repeated several times during the spacecraft's mission to land a man on the moon. Flipping the switch started a "stir" of the service module's Number 2 oxygen tank. Stirring the tank prevented liquid oxygen from turning gummy, and ensured a proper burn when oxygen mixed with fuel and was ignited.

Ninety-three seconds later, Swigert and his fellow astronauts, James Lovell and Fred Haise, heard an explosive *thump*. A shudder raked the command module. Lights flickered and monitors fluttered.

"Houston, we've had a problem here," James Lovell announced.

In the control room at the National Aeronautics and Space Administration (NASA) station in Houston, Texas, lights on an instrument console flashed. An alarm sounded. Engineers and technicians scrambled. Three days into its mission, Apollo 13 was in trouble.

At first the astronauts thought a meteor might have struck the spacecraft. They changed their minds after looking out the window. "It looks to me that we are venting something," Lovell told the ground crew. "It's a gas of some kind."

The service module held fuel and oxygen tanks, propulsion and electrical systems, and supplies for the mission. Although the exact cause of the problem wasn't known until later, flipping the switch had started a chain reaction. An electrical short in the Number 2 oxygen tank sparked a fire, causing an explosion. The explosion ruptured the tank, blew out bolts in the service module, ripped off a hatch cover and fired debris into space. It damaged neighbouring oxygen tanks and disabled power systems. Pushed by the force of the explosion, Apollo veered off course.

There was momentary silence in Houston as the news sunk in. The astronauts were marooned partway between Earth and the moon, without propulsion or electrical power and with only about two hours of oxygen left in the cabin.

In Houston, technicians and experts huddled, sharing ideas. Salvaging the command module and securing the safety of the astronauts became first priorities. The command module housed the crew's quarters and the equipment needed for re-entry. Without it, there would be no way to come home.

To extend the life of the command module's systems, Houston ordered them powered down. The astronauts moved into the lunar module, a cramped space smaller than a compact car. Nicknamed Aquarius but also fondly known as "the lifeboat," the lunar module was designed to land two of the astronauts on the moon's surface and return them to the orbiting command module afterward. It had independent systems — its own oxygen, fuel and engines.

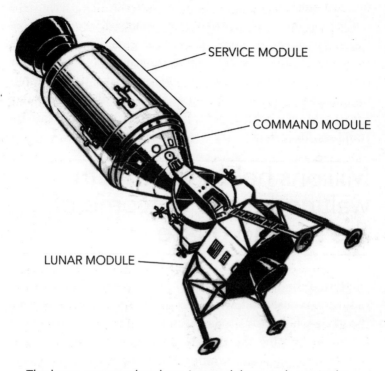

The lunar, command and service modules are shown in the docked position, prior to separation.

With the astronauts safely lodged in the lunar module, discussions turned to the larger issue: how to return the astronauts to Earth. A black void 321,800 kilometres wide separated the crippled spacecraft from home. What options did Houston have?

Engineers and technicians read manuals, searching for information and clues. They consulted experts with specialized skills and knowledge — people who understood Apollo and the ways of space travel. Heads together, they tossed out suggestions and debated the risks while the clock counted down minutes, then hours.

One option soon rose above the others. Known as a free trajectory return, it relied on multiple bursts of power from the lunar module descent engines to send Apollo into lunar orbit, swing it around the moon and then rocket the spaceship back to Earth. The descent engines were intended for one-time use. Could they handle multiple firings? Not even the experts could say for certain.

Millions held their breath, waiting for the outcome of the second phase.

Around the world, people gathered around televisions and radios, nervously following the story. Relief spread around the globe when the astronauts initiated the first phase of the sequence, burning the descent engines just enough to correct Apollo's flight and sending it into lunar orbit. As Apollo rounded the far side of the moon, millions held their breath, waiting for the outcome of the second phase. Would the engines fire again?

In the lunar module, the astronauts checked gauges and screens, their fingers on switches, ready for Houston's instructions. As Apollo zipped around the moon, Earth swept into view again. *Now!* There was a surge, a short burst of speed as the descent engines ignited, providing power enough to push Apollo out of lunar orbit and slingshot it to Earth.

Cheers erupted in Houston, and across the globe people celebrated. Apollo was on its way home, racing against dwindling supplies.

There were other hurdles to cross, more jittery moments. Designed for two men, not three, the lunar module was ill-equipped to handle an extra person. With each breath, the three astronauts expelled water vapour and carbon dioxide. Without power to operate heaters, temperatures plunged. Water condensed on wires and instruments, and threatened to short-out the module's power systems.

While the lunar module had replenishable stores of oxygen, it only had two lithium hydroxide canisters or "scrubbers" to clean the air of carbon dioxide. Now, with an extra person aboard, the scrubbers barely kept pace. A shortage of interchangeable round filters that fit the scrubbers compounded the problem. As Apollo shot home, carbon dioxide levels spiked and air quality rapidly deteriorated.

At ground control in Houston, engineers met around long tables, conscious that time was running out. Without additional filters — or a creative alternative — the astronauts would die of their own waste gases before Apollo reached Earth.

The engineers at Houston were young — their average age just twenty-six — but they were buoyed with hope and ideas. With just twenty-four hours to deal with the problem, they pitched solutions and judged their likelihood of success, knowing that three lives were at stake.

Ed Smylie, head of the Crew Systems Division, offered an idea. The command module had plenty of filters. Unfortunately, they were square, not round like those needed in the lunar module.

Was there a way to adapt the square filters from the command module and make them fit the round canisters in the lunar module? Smylie, with the help of his assistant Jim Correale, gathered materials the crew had on board — plastic bags, cardboard book covers, duct tape, fans and hoses ripped from astronaut suits.

From the supplies on hand, a contraption grew, cut from spare parts and spliced together with duct tape by Smylie and Correale. It looked flimsy and awkward — a funnel-like box with a chunk of hose that had a fan connected to a square filter.

The crew in Houston check out their "mailbox" adaptor before sending ideas to the astronauts.

Ground control crew christened the device "the mailbox." They ran it through a few tests, blowing air through the mailbox and measuring its effectiveness. Convinced it would work on the spacecraft, they radioed instructions to the astronauts. Within an hour, the astronauts had built a similar device from spare parts aboard Apollo. With square filters modified to replace round ones, they connected the mailbox and turned the scrubbers on.

"The contraption wasn't handsome, but it worked," James Lovell wrote in *Lost Moon*, his memoir about the event.

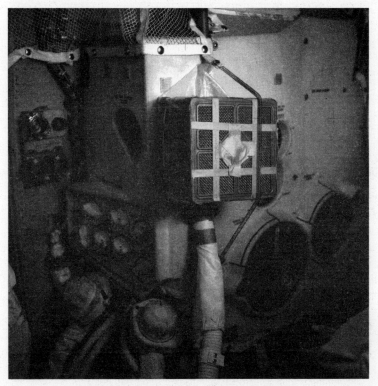

The astronauts' version of the "mailbox."

With the carbon dioxide situation under control, attention shifted to re-entry. It was a complicated process involving multiple steps — aligning the command module, adjusting its angle of entry and then harnessing the Earth's gravity to ride through the atmosphere.

Having the correct angle of entry was critical. Too shallow an angle and the capsule would skip off the atmosphere, much like a stone skips across a pond. Too steep and it would burn up from excessive friction on the way down.

To complicate matters, debris from the explosion had obscured the astronauts' view of the stars. Without stars or computers to guide Apollo, the astronauts were essentially flying blind. The only way home was to rely on gut instinct and years of experience to manually steer the spacecraft. Without navigational aids, it would be like driving a car at top speed with closed eyes.

From desperation grew a bold idea, something talked about, but never tried before. Why not use the Earth's terminator as a direction finder? The terminator — the shifting line on Earth that divides it into regions of night and day — can be seen from space. Using the sun as one marker, the terminator as another, and with the help of a watch and some geometry, could they guide Apollo home?

With Earth in sight and ground control issuing advice, the astronauts worked together to steer their vessel through a manual burn. Lovell controlled the "yaw" — movements left and right. Haise controlled the "pitch" — movements up and down. Swigert used his watch to time when the engine should be turned on or off.

It was, as one engineer put it, "a backup 'seat of the pants' means of navigating." But it worked. The engine burn was successful. The astronauts corrected the re-entry angle. Then, in preparation for landing, they moved into the command module.

Four-and-a-half hours before re-entry, the astronauts

jettisoned the service module. As the module slowly receded, they caught a glimpse of the damage made by the earlier explosion. "There's one whole side of that spacecraft missing," they reported to ground control. "A whole panel has blown out. Almost from the base to the engine. It's really a mess."

Two hours later, the astronauts tried starting the command module engines. Was there enough power left to fire them up?

Oxygen met fuel in the command module engines. A spark ignited the mix. Lights flickered on the control panel as systems returned to life. The astronauts were a step closer to coming home.

An hour later, the lunar module was jettisoned, too. "Farewell, Aquarius, and we thank you," ground control said over the radio.

Too steep an angle and the capsule would burn up from excessive friction.

At the precise angle needed for re-entry, the command module shot into Earth's atmosphere. At 1:07 p.m. on April 17, the capsule splashed down in the South Pacific, 142 hours and 54 minutes after the explosion. Plucked from their bobbing spacecraft, the astronauts were safe — heroes around the globe for their steely nerves and incredible determination. Just as heroic and even more persistent were the engineers and technicians at Mission Control in Houston. Toiling behind the scenes from a base thousands of kilometres away, they had improvised and invented, overcoming one problem after another to bring the astronauts home.

While on his lunch break at a railyard outside Toledo, Ohio, switchmaster Jon Hosfeld heard a radio message from the control tower: "I think we've got a problem."

An unmanned train towing forty-seven cars was steaming down the tracks, gaining speed. Two of the cars carried molten phenol, a poisonous chemical used in paint thinners. Somehow an engineer had applied the throttle instead of the brakes before stepping off the train. Now it was on the loose with its lethal cargo.

Hosfeld hopped aboard a truck with a co-worker, Mike Smith. While police cleared crossings in towns ahead, and supervisors in Toledo tried to derail the runaway train safely, the two men gave chase, barrelling down Interstate 75 at speeds close to 160 kilometres per hour.

When attempts to derail the train failed, supervisors sent another train after it, hoping to catch the runaway from behind, hook up to it, and by braking hard, slow it down. Meanwhile Hosfeld and Smith raced ahead, trying to beat the runaway before it entered Kenton, Ohio, a town with a steep downgrade and sharp curves.

When the second train caught up to the first, it attached and braked as planned, slowing down the runaway . . . but not enough. Still travelling at unsafe speeds, the runaway train neared Kenton. By then, Hosfeld and Smith were there, waiting at a crossing with Hosfeld outside the truck, ready to run. "I had only one chance," he said.

As the train swept by, Hosfeld took two quick steps, grabbed the railing with both hands and hoisted himself aboard. Swiftly he shut the throttle off, set the brakes and brought the runaway to a halt.

"It's over, fellas," he radioed Toledo. "I got it stopped. We're safe."

OUTSMARTING THE IMPOSSIBLE
May 5, 2001 / Queensland, Australia

During army training exercises, a tank occupied by a three-person crew suddenly veered out of control after a gun swung free, striking the driver, who had raised his head to see better. Corporal Shaun Clements jumped out of the turret and crept across the hull of the tank to reach the unconscious driver, whose foot was pressed against the accelerator.

As the tank sped through a wooded gully, Clements shielded the driver from falling branches and tried to regain control. Holding the driver's head in one hand, he pulled on the hand brakes with the other and tried, unsuccessfully, to reach the ignition switch to turn off the engine.

With the tank picking up speed, Clements saw two stationary tanks at the bottom of the gully, directly in the runaway's path. He wrestled with the steering mechanism and narrowly missed one of the stationary tanks, but his tank plowed on, seemingly unstoppable.

Then he spotted opportunity ahead — a steep, wooded slope that ran alongside the gully. Perhaps gravity could do what the braking system couldn't. He aimed for the uphill slope, and used gravity and the surrounding trees to slow down the tank and eventually stop it.

"I was just doing my job, I suppose," Clements said. "I just did what I had to do. I didn't have time to think about being scared or whatever."

For his brave, quick-thinking actions, Corporal Shaun Clements was awarded the Star of Courage, one of Australia's highest honours.

ANYWHERE, ANYTIME

In the dead of the Antarctic winter, there were no flights in, no flights out.

In Antarctica, winter arrives in February and lasts as late as October. At the Amundsen-Scott South Pole Research Station, 50 or more scientists, engineers and technicians hunker down in the Dome, a sprawling geodesic canopy that covers a dozen structures where "Polies" live and work.

Winter means isolation. For up to six months, Polies have only each other for company. There are no flights in or out of

Antarctica, no deliveries of fresh supplies, no visitors to engage in conversation. With temperatures sinking as low as minus 100° Celsius, airplane fuel turns to jelly, hydraulics fail and landing gears seize — it's just too dangerous to fly.

In February 2001 Ron Shemenski, the station's newly appointed doctor, arrived on one of the last flights of the season. "We're going to have a nice, quiet time," he told a colleague.

Two months later Dr. Shemenski doubled over in pain. He passed a gallstone, a sign of something dangerous stirring inside his abdomen. Gallstones can clog up the pancreatic duct, allowing digestive juices to get inside the pancreas, poisoning the system. Suddenly the Dome's quiet world turned upside down. The doctor had pancreatitis, a life-threatening condition requiring emergency surgery.

The entrance to the research station.

By this time Antarctica was in full lockdown. With Dr. She-menski gravely ill, the situation was serious, not only for him, but for the entire mission. He was the station's only doctor. Who would look after the others if he couldn't? And with all flights cancelled, how would he get the medical help he desperately required?

An urgent call went to the headquarters of the South Pole base in Denver, Colorado. Experts pored over maps and weather charts, contemplating their options. There was really only one. A plane carrying an experienced crew would have to brave the Antarctic winter, with its unpredictable winds and blinding blizzards, to fly in another doctor and then fly Dr. Shemenski out afterward.

The US Air Force and National Guard readied three LC-130 Hercules cargo planes and 50 military personnel. The planes waited on the tarmac in Christchurch, New Zealand, for weather conditions at the South Pole to improve. Hercules aircraft cannot operate below minus 55° Celsius, and already temperatures at the research station had dipped lower. Long-range forecasts predicted even worse conditions.

Denver scrapped the Hercules plan. Even if one of the giant airplanes landed successfully, there was no guarantee it would be able to fly out later. Dr. Shemenski, his replacement and the flight crew would all be stranded until October.

Then someone remembered Kenn Borek Air, a Canadian firm stationed in Calgary, Alberta, that flew rugged bush planes into the Far North. The company's motto was *Anytime, Anywhere . . . Worldwide.* Perhaps it could help.

True to their motto, Kenn Borek accepted the challenge. Within hours, a plan was in place. Two Twin Otter airplanes stood ready in Calgary, engines primed and purring, each manned by an experienced crew of three.

Compared to the Hercules, the eight-seater, Canadian-built Twin Otter was small and compact, a prop-driven plane with a reputation for rugged durability. Rated safe for temperatures as low as minus 75° Celsius, it had been used for decades to fly people and cargo into and out of remote locations. But Antarctica in the dead of winter was something new.

Metal rods snapped from the cold; skis stuck like glue to the rough ice.

The two crews understood the challenge, the likelihood of trouble, the possibility of failure — metal rods snapping from the cold, fuel turning thick as paste, skis sticking like glue to the rough ice. Hours of flight experience had prepared them for challenging situations, but as the planes flew out of Calgary, doubts sifted through each crew member's mind.

"You start thinking about some of the possibilities that could happen and you want to make sure you plan for all the contingencies involved," Sean Loutitt, one of the pilots, said.

The two Twin Otters left Calgary on April 14 and leapfrogged over oceans and continents, first to Punta Arenas, Chile, then to a British research station, Rothera, on the Antarctic Peninsula. The plan was for one of the planes to make the 2080-kilometre flight from Rothera to the South Pole while the second plane waited at Rothera, backup for the first plane in case of trouble.

Loutitt was selected as the pilot of the first plane; Mark Cary as co-pilot. Both men had flown Twin Otters to far corners of the world. They knew the Twin Otter, its whims and wants, the ways to sweet talk it through rough times. To decide on who would be their flight engineer, they tossed a coin. Norman Wong, a skilled mechanic, won the toss to round out the crew.

To make the journey, they needed thirty-six hours of clear weather — ten hours to fly to the South Pole; ten hours to recover, catch up on sleep and service the plane; another ten hours to make the flight back again. In the pitch-blackness of a polar winter, they would be flying blind, relying on radar and delicate flight instruments to see what their eyes couldn't.

While meteorologists at the Amundsen-Scott base monitored the weather for clear skies and warmer conditions, crews dug out a 2-kilometre landing strip. In bitter cold, rubber becomes brittle and even the hardiest tractor can stall. Worried that the tractor treads might snap, crews worked carefully in the dark, coaxing frozen machines to life, slowly carving a runway out of the ice.

Meanwhile, carpenters and mechanics constructed smudge pots to light the landing strip. A number of 200-litre oil drums sliced in half were filled with mixtures of wood and gasoline, and then placed alongside the runway. Set on fire with propane torches, the smudge pots would be flaming cauldrons, easily sighted in the dark.

After three days the weather in Rothera improved. A tiny window of opportunity opened, enough to send the Twin Otter crew to the station. And so began a flight like no other before it. With Dr. Betty Carlisle, the replacement physician, aboard, the Twin Otter and its crew took to the air.

Four hours into the flight, the weather soured. Winds broadsided the plane, snow pelted it and temperatures dived. The crew were not yet halfway. There was still time to change their minds. But the pilots forged ahead. They had encountered turbulence before. They had blasted through blizzards thick as cotton. They would do the same now.

Ten hours later the Twin Otter crew sighted a dozen

glowing lights — the flaming smudge pots marking the runway.

"To finally see what you're looking for and to be able to identify it, that was an extremely special moment," co-pilot Cary said. "It was very poetic actually to arrive at the bottom of the world, in a land that's covered in ice and snow, to these glowing barrels of burning debris."

Guided by the smudge pots, Loutitt and Cary landed the plane and taxied down the runway, skis clattering on the bumpy ice. Polies waiting with snowmobiles took over. After a frigid 2-kilometre ride to the Dome, the Twin Otter crew and replacement doctor arrived at the research station to warmth, food and much-needed rest.

The Twin Otter arrives at the Amundsen-Scott South Pole Station.

Temperatures hovered around minus 69° Celsius, dangerously close to the mark where even hardy Twin Otters run into trouble. While the crew rested, mechanics placed heaters around the plane. They also bundled the engine in protective covers to keep fluids thin and prevent metal from snapping. Although the mission was more than half over, the most difficult leg was still coming.

Weather ruled the timeline. While the crew snuggled inside the Dome, winds picked up and temperatures dropped.

What was to be a ten-hour recovery period stretched longer as they waited for conditions to improve. Finally, after a delay of several hours, the weather shifted again. Once more a small window of opportunity opened. Anxious to take advantage of it, the Twin Otter crew headed to the plane.

The engines growled to life, but there were problems. For one, the skis had frozen into the ice. The crew repositioned the heaters, aimed them at the skis and, armed with shovels, chipped and chopped the melting ice to set them free.

The flaps along the wings had frozen, too. Flaps control lift. With flaps locked into the fully extended position, even if the plane travelled at top speed it would not get enough lift to leave the runway.

Engineer Norman Wong walked around the wings. He was a problem-solver with years of flight experience. He knew the Twin Otter better than anyone. If there was a way, he'd find it.

With odds and ends of wire and cable, Wong figured out a way to rig the flaps so they could be raised and lowered, making them operational again.

"You get a heightened awareness," Wong said when describing the moment. "Time seems to slow down and you just focus on the problem and what you need to accomplish."

With Dr. Ron Shemenski aboard, the plane rumbled down the runway, slowly gaining speed for liftoff. As the smudge pots disappeared from view, the plane sliced through the dark and swept toward home.

In the cockpit, the pilots monitored the instrument panel. Frost covered the dials. Needles froze into fixed positions. Unable to rely on their instruments, the men hoped that they were going in the right direction, but in the dark there was no way to know for certain.

Finally a sign appeared. "All of a sudden," Mark Cary said,

"there was this faint pink line on the horizon. It was really beautiful to watch it grow. It was like a gift and a sign to say everything's going to work out and you guys are going the right way."

Guided by the sun, the Twin Otter aimed for Rothera. When they landed at 8:52 p.m. on April 25, 2001, Dr. Ron Shemenski was one step closer to getting life-saving surgery. The crew, meanwhile, entered the history books. It was the first time that a plane had landed at the South Pole and then taken off again during an Antarctic winter.

THIRTY-THREE OF US

**A new sound echoed through the mine —
the drone of drills chewing through rock.**

Deep inside Chile's San Jose Mine, shift supervisor Luis Urzua felt the earth quiver. It was 2:00 p.m. on Tuesday, August 5, 2010. Urzua was five hours into his shift, directing miners 600 metres below the surface. Until then the day had been routine — thirty-three miners hard at work drilling through rock, seeking deposits of copper and gold in the maze of tunnels underground.

Moments after the tremor an explosion rocked the mine. A wave of compressed air blasted down the tunnel, knocking some of the men off their feet. Toxic dust shot through shafts and tunnels. Cloaked in a cloud of silt, the miners struggled just to breathe.

Urzua immediately realized the seriousness of the situation. The San Jose Mine was a honeycomb of unstable galleries and interconnected shafts. Weakened by erosion and years of drilling, one of the fragile upper corridors had collapsed, loosening tonnes of rock. The rockfall had plugged the ramp that coiled through the mine, blocking their route back to the surface.

Although the men had been working in different locations inside the mine, the blast drew them together. They abandoned their trucks and drilling equipment. Unable to go up, they went deeper into the mine, aiming for a small emergency room, about the size of five parking stalls, that had a reinforced ceiling.

It took an hour for some to reach the emergency room. They arrived caked in dust and fighting for air. Once all were inside, the metal doors were closed to block out the dust. Taking turns breathing from oxygen tanks, the men waited while Urzua counted their supplies: 10 litres of water, 16 litres of milk, 18 litres of juice, 96 packets of crackers, an assortment of canned tuna, peaches, peas and beans. Under normal circumstances, these would keep a crew of ten alive for forty-eight hours. But there were thirty-three men crammed into the small space. Who knew how long they would have to stay there.

The miners had no idea when rescue might come . . . *if* it came.

Outside the mine, workers heard the explosion. There was no sign of Urzua and his crew, no word from below. Reporters, cameramen and curiosity seekers converged on the site, eager for news. Families of the trapped men arrived, too. Soon a small community rose above the Chilean desert, a patchwork quilt of tents, tarps, trailers and motorhomes. Someone dubbed it Camp Hope. The name stuck. Camp Hope it was.

Rock experts were called — engineers, geologists, geophysicists; men and women who knew the mine and its fickle ways. The team examined its options. Was there a way to reach the men? A way to bring them back to the surface?

Ventilation shafts riddled the mine, bringing fresh air below. Why not use the shafts to reach the miners, someone suggested. But when they tried, they found the shafts plugged with rock. The rescue team explored other alternatives. Some were too risky, others too complicated or lengthy. Finally, just one remained: *drill*. Bore a small hole 700 metres deep through the rock to locate the miners. Once they were found, drill a larger hole, wide enough to fit a man. Then haul the miners up one by one.

It was more difficult than it sounded. Although the drilling technique had been used to rescue miners in Pennsylvania a few years before, it had never been used in such a large-scale operation. Not with thirty-three men. Not to such a depth, and not in a mine as fragile or complicated as this, with more than 6 kilometres of tunnels snaking through the earth. Drilling might unleash more rock, sealing the men inside forever.

* * *

Inside the mine, temperatures averaged 33° Celsius. Combined with dust and high humidity, the air was hard to breathe. Sweat streaming down their blackened faces, the miners removed shirts, loosened belts and stripped down to their underwear.

Given the circumstances, it would have been easy to surrender to chaos. But the miners knew that survival depended on teamwork. Democratic rules were established. With all miners participating, decisions were discussed and debated. All angles considered, the men voted. A majority — sixteen or more votes in favour — carried a decision.

Food was the most pressing matter. To make their sparse supplies last, the men voted to eat only two meals a day — tiny portions, one every twelve hours. They established other rules, too. They would eat together as a family, and not one person could taste a bite until all had been served.

Rescue, if it came at all, might be weeks away.

To keep the men busy and productive, duties were assigned. Some scouted the mine's many tunnels looking for possible escape routes. Others maintained equipment, scraped rock from the roof to prevent further collapse, or tended to other miners too weak or ill to do much for themselves.

"We worked as a team to keep morale up," Mario Sepulveda, one of the miners, said.

Rescue, if it came at all, might be weeks away. Until then, the small shelter served as home base. Buried deep in every miner's mind, though, was another thought — that the shelter might become their tomb.

* * *

On Day 4 drilling began. Cranes, bulldozers and dozens of vehicles large and small dotted the mine site. Guided by digital maps, engineers started nine separate holes, each one aimed at a spot where the men might have taken refuge. A vehicle workshop below the caved-in area was one. The small emergency room lower down was another. Tunnels and shafts sturdy and large enough to shelter men became the other seven sites.

The boreholes were small, about the size of baseballs. Even with drill bits whirling at high speed, it would take at least a week to hit one of the targets. If the rescuers encountered problems, it might take even longer.

Rescue teams worked feverishly, not knowing if the boreholes would ever be used. There had been no sign of the miners, no indication that they were still alive.

* * *

With food rations rapidly dwindling, the miners held a meeting. To extend their supplies, they voted to eat only one meal a day.

On Day 5 a new sound echoed through the tunnels. It was faint and distant, but unmistakeable — the drone of drills chewing through rock. The miners cheered and celebrated. Rescuers were on their way.

The men adjusted their timeline, stretching out the meagre food supply to last longer. On Day 9 they cut their portions again. Instead of eating once a day, they ate once every thirty-six hours. More than ever, they kept busy. One of the men made a set of dominoes out of a safety triangle. Another dismantled the seats from a truck and converted them into a comfortable bed. Groups took long walks down corridors. Some gathered in circles, sharing dreams and fears. Food was a frequent topic, with vivid descriptions of tasty meals they would one day enjoy again.

Motivated by the possibility of rescue, the men thought ahead. If a drill bit punctured the roof of the mine, they would need to be ready. They wrote messages. They gathered cans of orange spray paint. The plan was simple. Once the bit punctured a tunnel, they would paint the drill shaft bright orange and tie messages to the bit. When the bit was retracted and raised, rescuers would know the truth: thirty-three miners were down there, all alive and eager to be reunited with their families.

On Day 16 the men cut their food portions again. There were only two cans of tuna left. Meals became one bite for each miner every three days. Exhaustion set into their starving bodies. Even so they rehearsed their plan. The cans of paint were ready.

* * *

The drilling above continued, but slower than expected. Called upon by Chilean president Sebastian Piñera, experts from other countries, including Canada and the United States, gave advice. If and when the miners were located, it would take weeks to drill another hole large enough to bring up the men. In the meantime, the miners would need support.

Rescuers were venturing into uncharted territory. . . . Were the miners even still alive?

Specialists drew on their strengths and know-how to develop plans for the future. Never before had there been a rescue of miners from such depths — not from such a fragile mine, and not after such a long period underground. Rescuers were venturing into uncharted territory, trying what had never been tried before.

Doctors, nutritionists and other health experts considered the miners' physical and mental state, and the food, vitamins, inoculations, exercise and psychological support they might require. To talk with the miners, communication expert Pedro Gallo built a tiny telephone to drop down the small borehole.

To transfer supplies to the men, physics professor Miguel Fortt developed the *paloma*, a system of 3-metre-long tubes that could be linked together and lowered down the same shaft. At the same time, engineers worked on Phoenix, a rocket-shaped capsule large enough to transport a single person up to the surface.

On Day 17 at 5:30 a.m. one of the drills suddenly spun free, offering no further resistance. Drilling teams rejoiced. The bit had hit a hollow space 690 metres below the surface. But was this where the miners were located? Were they even still alive?

* * *

Below, the miners fanned through the mine, tracking the sound of crashing rock and whirring drills. When they found the exposed bit, there was chaos. "It was crazy," one of the miners said. "People were running everywhere."

True to the plan, they worked quickly, spraying the drill shaft with orange paint and attaching the messages with an elastic band torn from one man's underwear. For over an hour they banged the shaft to alert rescuers, and then they watched with relief when the bit slowly rose and disappeared.

On the surface, workers found the orange paint and shredded notes. *Estaos Bien En El Reguio los 33*, one of them said. *We are all right in the shelter, the thirty-three of us.*

Camp Hope burst into celebration. A tiny remote-controlled camera was lowered down the borehole and soon the world was watching what seemed impossible — thirty-three men on the brink of starvation, clad in tatters, hugging each other.

Within hours, the *paloma* system of tubes was in place shuttling bottled water, food, the telephone and other communication devices to the men. The focus of the rescue changed. The men had been located. Now they had to be brought up to the surface. It meant drilling a wider hole through the rock to haul them up, a job that could take many weeks, maybe even months.

Monster drilling machines on loan from Australia, the United States and Canada rolled into place. To offset the risk of collapse, three large holes were started, each aimed at a different location. Phoenix, the bullet-like rescue capsule, was tested and refined. The lives of the men depended on the 420-kilogram capsule slipping through the hole, riding up and down on its retractable wheels without fail.

The rescue capsule — Phoenix.

With rescue teams advising the miners, the men entered a new phase of captivity underground. To give the miners purpose and a sense of normalcy, new rules and routines were established. The tunnels were flooded with light to simulate cycles of day and night. Grouped into three teams, the men worked eight-hour shifts, unloading the *paloma*, shoring up walls and patrolling tunnels to clear them of debris. One of the men carried a hand-held computerized device that transmitted oxygen, carbon dioxide and air temperature readings to experts above.

To keep the men fit, professional athletes led the miners through exercises. Some of the men went a step further and took to jogging a 5-kilometre circuit through the tunnels. Daily video conferences kept the men in touch with family. Through it all the world watched as, each day, drills pulverized the rock.

On Day 65 one of the drills broke through the roof of the vehicle workshop, creating a 70-centimetre-wide shaft to the surface. Over the next two days, surface workers stabilized the borehole and made adjustments to Phoenix. The capsule, 2 metres high on the inside, was equipped with a video camera and intercom system. Its retractable wheels were oiled, the springs adjusted. Lights were installed inside to illuminate the rock wall as it slid through the opening. To test the device and ready the miners, five rescue workers rode down the bumpy shaft.

After 69 days underground, rescue day finally came for the miners. They donned green jumpsuits, tailor-made for a streamlined fit.

First to go up was Florencio Avalos. Wearing long stretch socks to help with circulation, a girdle to make him as compact as possible and sunglasses to protect his eyes from the harsh sun, Avalos stepped into the capsule at 11:53 p.m. on Tuesday, October 12, 2011. Fifteen minutes later he emerged on the surface to cheering crowds and an estimated one billion viewers who were watching the rescue on television. After shaking hands with President Piñera and hugging his family, Avalos was wheeled away on a stretcher to a nearby field hospital.

One by one, the men were brought to the surface. The last miner up was Luis Urzua. "Mr. President," he said simply, "my shift is over."

It *was* over, and the miners had set a world record — the longest confinement underground of any mine survivors.

STRANDED

Without warning the weather soured, trapping the two men in an Arctic blizzard.

For the two Inuit hunters, conditions near the hamlet of Igloolik off the coast of Canada's Baffin Island were perfect for hunting. That Wednesday, October 26, 2011, the wind was calm, and Foxe Basin a carpet of quiet waves. With any luck, they'd spot a walrus, a primary food source in the Arctic.

From Igloolik, seventeen-year-old Lester Aqqiaruq and his father, David, launched their open aluminum boat. Ninety minutes later they caught a walrus. There was little time to celebrate, however. Before long the weather soured. The wind rose. Temperatures plunged and snow fell. Angry waves slammed the boat and the sea turned slushy. Soon the boat was surrounded by pack ice and the two hunters were trapped in an Arctic blizzard.

Lester and his father had a SPOT beacon with them, an electronic device that broadcasts an emergency signal when activated. Around 9:00 p.m. they switched it on. Stranded, they huddled around a small camp stove in the moonless night. They waited, chilled and wet, drawing hope from the flickering flame and from each other. Had the signal reached someone?

Rescue, if it came at all to this remote place, would be hours away. No search and rescue aircraft were based in the Arctic, only in more populated regions of southern Canada, thousands of kilometres away.

* * *

That night the signal reached the Rescue Coordination Centre (RCC) in Trenton, Ontario. Officials checked their inventory of available planes at bases across Canada, looking for one to fly north and check on the situation. They found one — a Hercules transport — sitting on the tarmac in Winnipeg.

A brute of a plane, the Hercules had four turboprop engines, a large cargo bay and a reputation for rugged durability. It could take off and land on short, uneven runways. Fully fuelled, it could fly long distances without stopping, too.

A quickly assembled crew hurried to the plane, threw supplies aboard and fired the engines. While most of Winnipeg slept, the plane roared down the runway. In minutes it was aloft, flying northeast, homing in on the SPOT beacon signal.

At 3:50 a.m. the plane swept over the scene. Through the driving snow, the crew spotted the small boat and its two tiny figures. The boat was locked in ice about 10 kilometres from shore. There was no nearby place to land the plane. In these conditions, not even boats launched from Igloolik could reach them.

The Hercules crew radioed the RCC base in Trenton that they had located the men. They knew more about their situation, about the ice surrounding them, the screaming wind and thrashing waves. The Hercules would continue to monitor the situation, but without refuelling, it couldn't fly forever. More than a single plane would be needed to pluck the Aqqiaruqs from the swollen sea.

Hearing the news, emergency officials in Trenton re-evaluated the situation. Any kind of Arctic rescue pushes resources to the limit. Because of its remote location and the unpredictable weather, this one was especially tricky and dangerous. To save the two hunters, rescue crews would have to adapt to ever-shifting conditions, modifying their plans at a moment's notice.

While the Winnipeg Hercules continued to fly over Lester and David Aqqiaruq, RCC officials dispatched two more aircraft. From Trenton a second Hercules, this one equipped with rescue gear, relief supplies and three experienced search and rescue (SAR) technicians. From Gander, Newfoundland, a Cormorant helicopter carrying a rescue crew of five.

A Cormorant rescue helicopter from Canada's fleet flies over the North Atlantic.

Time was the critical factor. The hunters had already been stranded more than twelve hours. Even travelling at top speed, the second Hercules would not arrive until sometime in the afternoon. The Cormorant would take much longer. By the time it arrived, it would be evening, almost a full day since the stranded pair had activated the beacon.

Forecasts called for worsening weather. Things were getting worse for Lester and his father.

* * *

In their open boat, the Aqqiaruqs bucked ice-capped waves. They watched the Hercules thunder overhead, making one futile pass after another. Their hopes dwindled with each drone of the engines. "I thought we were going to die," Lester said.

Around 3:00 p.m. on Thursday afternoon, the second Hercules arrived to take the place of the one from Winnipeg. Unable to land nearby or to rescue the men, the crew dropped a phone to the hunters. Unfortunately, it landed far away. The Aqqiaruqs couldn't reach it.

On subsequent passes the Hercules dropped a radio and two rescue kits containing a camp stove, provisions and a six-person life raft. These landed closer. The hunters climbed aboard the raft, their icy fingers gripping slippery rubber. Shortly afterward the aluminum boat sank, taking all of their gear with it. Within minutes the radio died, too.

By now hypothermia had set in, slowing their reactions. They tried lighting the camp stove, but it was too wet. There was food aboard, but they couldn't open the packages. "Our hands were really cold," Lester said.

Aboard the second Hercules, the crew discussed options. Weather conditions, both winds and waves, were deteriorating. The Cormorant chopper skirting up the coast wouldn't arrive for hours. The hunters would not survive without immediate help.

With daylight fading, SAR techs Marco Journeyman, Maxime Lahaye-Lemay and Janick Gilbert donned parachutes. Without a working radio, communication with the plane would be lost once they hit the water. Instead, they agreed to use the personal beacon locators each one carried. One beacon activated told the flight crew that they were all okay; two meant they were in trouble.

The Passages route was shorter . . . but more dangerous, too.

In the dark, the three men leaped from the plane. One landed close to the raft and climbed aboard. A second landed farther away. Unable to fight the waves, he deployed the one-man raft he carried and climbed inside. The third SAR tech, Janick Gilbert, was blown off course by high winds.

One beacon flashed. Then a second. To the crew aboard the Hercules, the message was clear. Five men, not just two, were now in trouble.

* * *

Powered by three engines, the Cormorant chopped along the Atlantic coast carrying its crew of five: Aaron Noble, the commander; Dean Vey, the co-pilot; Brad Hiscock, the flight engineer; and two search and rescue technicians, Daniel Villeneuve and Shawn Bretschneider.

Time was evaporating. Almost twelve hours into its mission, a call came over the radio updating the men about the SAR crew in trouble. In the Cormorant, options were considered. The route that the chopper followed up the Atlantic coast was near refuelling stops, but long and meandering. Was there a faster way to reach the site?

The answer was there, staring at the Cormorant crew from maps and electronic screens. If they abandoned the safety of the shoreline and flew directly over the broad, stormy waters of Northwestern Passages instead, they could shave off an hour, maybe more. Although the Passages route was shorter, it was more dangerous, too. But five men were at risk, bobbing in uncertain seas, and who else could come to their rescue in a place so remote?

It took just a few minutes to decide. "We'll be doing what we can to get these guys out of the water," the chopper crew radioed the RCC base. "We're proceeding direct at this time."

Steering northwest, the chopper flew directly over water, buffeted by strong winds and shrouded in cloud cover. At the RCC base in Trenton, officials monitored the flight. They kept in close radio contact, knowing that if the helicopter ran into difficulty, there would be little they could do. If another helicopter had to be dispatched, it would take at least twelve hours more to get there.

At 9:46 p.m. the RCC radio crackled with good news. The Cormorant had arrived at the site. Relief was short-lived, though. Weather conditions were far worse than expected — wind gusts up to 80 kilometres per hour, waves 10 metres tall. Descending below the clouds, the Cormorant crew spotted beacon lights blinking in multiple locations. Some were clustered close together, others far away. Each one marked an object tossed by the sea. Instead of a single drop to the ice to rescue the two hunters, many more might be needed.

The Cormorant hovered over one life raft with Hiscock manning the hoist. Paying out cable, he lowered Villeneuve and Bretschneider into the water.

Dragging a hoist hook and a rescue "horse collar," Villeneuve and Bretschneider swam to the life raft. Three men were inside, a SAR tech with the Aqqiaruqs, all on the brink of collapse. One after the other, the horse collar was fastened around the men. One after the other, they were hoisted into the helicopter.

We have ... one possible black.

While Villeneuve tended to the three men, the chopper crept to a second life raft. Again Bretschneider was lowered into the sea. A second SAR tech was extracted and hauled aboard, chilled but grateful.

Where was the third SAR tech? Multiple blinking beacons pitched on the waves. Two were attached to empty life rafts. Another was attached to a floating helmet. Then the crew spotted a glint in the dark . . . light reflecting off the ice, they thought. But when the helicopter zeroed in for a closer look, they saw Janick Gilbert bobbing on the waves. He'd been in the water for five hours.

Again Bretschneider was lowered. Gilbert was unconscious and as Bretschneider wrestled with the horse collar, the heavy hoist hook struck his head. Dazed, he still managed to hook Gilbert's body to the hoist. Then he attached himself.

With both men weighted on the line, Hiscock struggled to haul them aboard. The two other SAR techs, warmed now and partly recovered, lent a hand.

"We have all three SAR techs on board," the chopper crew radioed RCC Trenton as it headed to Igloolik. "We have . . . one possible black. We're going to need an ambulance immediately at the airport."

In the language of rescue, "black" is code. It means that a victim — Janick Gilbert, in this case — is in mortal danger, near death and in need of immediate medical attention.

At the Igloolik hospital, doctors treated the men. Journeyman and Lahaye-Lemay, the two rescued SAR techs, recovered. So, too, did Lester and David Aqqiaruq, who suffered from exposure and frostbite. Unfortunately, the third SAR tech, Janick Gilbert, did not. Despite attempts to resuscitate him, he was declared dead shortly after the helicopter arrived.

In 2012 the five-man crew of the Cormorant helicopter was selected for a special honour. To mark the men's heroic actions, they were chosen as the winners of the 2012 Cormorant Trophy for Helicopter Rescue.

LIFE OR DEATH
– LIBERATE

BEHIND THE BRICK WALL

Few knew about the well-kept secret or the lives it protected.

From the outside, the two-and-a-half-storey building standing at 19 Barteljorisstraat in the Harlem section of Amsterdam, the Netherlands, looked much like its neighbours. It was old and rambling, a jumble of rooms and hollow spaces with a watch shop on the main floor and living quarters above. The street was lined with other businesses, and the watch shop was just one more. Or so it seemed. Few knew about the dangerous mission operating there, the secrets inside or the small bedroom at the top of the staircase — Corrie ten Boom's bedroom — which, like the rest of the house, seemed so normal, but wasn't.

During World War II, when the Netherlands was occupied by Nazi Germany, forty-eight-year-old Corrie ten Boom, her sister Bessie and their father Caspar lived and worked at the building. To outsiders they appeared to be a quiet family, deeply religious, devoted to each other and hardly the troublemaking kind.

One day in 1941, German soldiers stormed the fur shop across the street, tossing clothes and personal items out the window and evicting its Jewish owner. Corrie and Bessie ten Boom ran to help their neighbour. They scooped up his belongings and brought him home. For the rest of the day, the ten Booms hid the man, waiting until darkness for the Dutch Resistance to smuggle him out.

It was a defiant act, born of compassion, and the beginning of something remarkable. Helping Jews was against the law, and hiding them an act punishable by death. Yet for Corrie ten Boom and her family, helping others was a way of life. Word of their kindness spread, and soon their house became a bustling place — a safe harbour for Jews and other refugees, and a centre for the Dutch Resistance.

During World War II, many Dutch worked in the underground Resistance, endangering their lives trying to bring an end to the German occupation. The Gestapo searched homes, relentlessly seeking out those loyal to the Resistance.

German police round up Jews in Amsterdam in February 1941.

Despite the danger, the ten Booms welcomed refugees and kept them hidden until safer quarters could be found. With so many mouths to feed and with so many strangers filtering through the *Beje* — Corrie ten Boom's nickname for the ten Boom home — keeping the operation secret from the Gestapo was difficult. A raid on the *Beje* was a strong possibility. Something had to be done.

After studying the configuration of rooms in the house, an architect with the Dutch Resistance, a man with the code name Mr. Smit, offered a suggestion.

"This is it," he said to Corrie ten Boom when he entered her small bedroom. It was the highest room in the house, the one farthest from the front door. Mr. Smit drew a line on the floor two paces from the back wall. "This is where the false wall will go."

In the six days that followed, a steady stream of "customers" flowed in and out of the *Beje*. They carried cleverly disguised items — hammers, trowels, bricks or mortar — hidden in briefcases, boxes or rolled-up newspapers. Working quietly and unnoticed, the Resistance team constructed a brick wall across the bedroom to create a secret room — a hiding place for "guests" should the Gestapo come calling.

The room was tiny, barely the size of a closet. Standing shoulder to shoulder, about a half-dozen people could hide there. To supply oxygen to the room, workers rigged up a ventilation system. They roughed up the brick on the outside to make the new wall look as old as others in the house, and installed a sagging bookcase in front. A sliding panel, 60 centimetres by 60 centimetres in the left-hand corner of the bookcase beneath the bottom shelf, became a hidden door. The room was equipped with emergency supplies — a jug of water, some hardtack biscuits, a mattress on the floor. Because it was constructed out of brick, the wall absorbed sounds and hid the hollowness behind.

Corrie ten Boom's bedroom, showing the false wall, bookshelf and hiding place.

"The Gestapo could search for a year," Mr. Smit said proudly of the room. "They'll never find this one."

Practice drills were held. A buzzer was installed at the top of the stairs, with push buttons to activate it situated at critical points around the house. When the buzzer sounded, guests scurried, picking up clothes, hiding cups and plates, and turning over mattresses to make sure that there was no "warm spot" for the Gestapo to feel. They crawled through the small opening in the bookcase with their belongings, closed the sliding panel and sandwiched their bodies inside. With enough practice, the whole process took little more than a minute.

Meanwhile, the ten Boom family practised routines of their

own. When the buzzer sounded, they threw a tablecloth over a table, set dishes in place and casually sat down, giving the impression that they were just having tea. They also rehearsed the answers they might give if questioned by the Gestapo.

For a year and a half, the ten Booms harboured refugees and lived dangerous double lives while Nazi security tightened. "Ostensibly we were still an elderly watchmaker living with his two spinster daughters above his tiny shop," Corrie ten Boom wrote later. "In actuality, the *Beje* was the centre of an underground ring that spread now to the farthest corners of Holland. Here daily came dozens of workers, reports, appeals. Sooner or later we were going to make a mistake."

The panel was slid into place just moments before a stranger burst into the room.

One Wednesday morning in February 1944, while Corrie ten Boom was ill with the flu, a stranger showed up at the house. The man claimed that he and his wife had been hiding Jews, but now his wife had been arrested.

"I need six hundred *guilders*," he told Corrie ten Boom. "I am told that you have certain contacts . . . "

The man spoke Dutch. He seemed sincere, but was he working for the Gestapo?

Despite her uneasiness, Corrie ten Boom felt compelled to help. "Come back in half an hour," she told him. "I'll have the money."

Minutes later the buzzer sounded, warning that infiltrators had entered the *Beje*. Six Jewish "guests" piled into the secret room. The panel was slid into place just moments before a stranger burst into the room, shouting, "So you are the ringleader! Now tell me where you are hiding the Jews."

Other men — some Gestapo, others Dutch supporters of the Nazi movement — swarmed through the *Beje*. They rounded up the family and a few legitimate visitors who happened to be there, corralled them in the living room and drilled them with questions.

"Where are the Jews?" one asked. "Where is the secret room?" He hit Corrie ten Boom repeatedly when she would not answer.

The men unsuccessfully searched the house, toppling furniture and smashing cupboards. If there was a secret room, they could not find it. Discouraged, but not willing to give up, the officer in charge stationed a guard outside the house. Sooner or later the "guests" would have to come out.

The ten Booms were arrested. They were questioned and beaten. The following day they were sent to a prison near Hague, a town 40 kilometres away. Separated from her family and confined to a cell of her own, Corrie ten Boom endured days of questioning and gave the answers she'd practised, never revealing information about the secret room or the people hiding there.

One day a guard threw a parcel into her cell. She found a few biscuits inside, a towel, needle and thread, and an envelope containing a note from her married sister, Nollie. The stamp on the envelope was crooked. Suspicious, Corrie ten Boom tore off the stamp to discover a tiny scrawled message underneath: *All the watches left in the cupboard are safe*, it said. The message was code for *The Jews in the room have escaped*.

For the remainder of the war, Corrie ten Boom was confined to prison cells and detainment centres in Holland and Germany. Her sister Bessie died. So did her father. But despite the hardships and close calls, Corrie ten Boom never revealed the information the Gestapo wanted.

After the war, Corrie ten Boom co-wrote *The Hiding Place*, a book about the secret room and her wartime experiences. Inspired by her faith, she toured various countries, spreading messages of forgiveness and renewal, until her death in 1983 at the age of 91.

Today the house at 19 Barteljorisstraat is a museum visited often by tourists. They come to the *Beje* to stand in the small bedroom at the highest point in the house, to see for themselves the brick wall and the secret panel, and to marvel at what Corrie ten Boom did while Nazi soldiers patrolled the street outside.

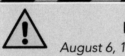

FACING THE IMPOSSIBLE
August 6, 1942 / Warsaw Ghetto, Poland

When German soldiers arrived at an orphanage with instructions to deport all 192 children and their caretakers to Treblinka, an extermination camp in Poland, Janusz Korczak faced a critical decision. He was the head of the orphanage, and a respected figure in Poland. He knew that the children were being sent to the gas chamber. For them, there would be no escape. Korczak, though, was offered a way out. Freedom could be his if he wanted it.

Korczak knew what lay ahead for the children — a long train ride in stifling boxcars; a terrifying countdown to death once they reached Treblinka. Rather than abandon the children, he volunteered to escort them to the camp, willingly choosing death for himself so the children would not die alone.

Korczak knew that if he acted calmly, if he modelled bravery, it would ease the children's anxiety on their final journey. He told the children to wear their best clothes and happiest faces, for they were leaving the dreary ghetto. Then, clutching a child's hand in each of his own, he led them out of the orphanage and guided them down the street to a waiting train 5 kilometres away.

Korczak, the children and their caretakers were never heard from again. His courageous act has not been forgotten, though. It lives on in numerous books, plays and films that tell his story, and in statues erected to his memory in Poland. It also lives on in the lesson Janusz Korczak taught us: When survival itself is not possible, how you face death may be the only choice left.

REACHING EVERY VILLAGE

The famine left little money for food, or to send William to school.

When the rains finally came, they were heavy, falling night and day for a week. In west Africa, great floods swept over Malawi, washing away homes, livestock and any seedlings that had sprouted. For months afterward, the sun blazed in a cloudless sky, baking the earth. Plants that survived the flood shrivelled and died. Famine followed. Then drought.

At the home in Masitala village where fourteen-year-old William Kamkwamba lived with his family, there was food on the table most days, even if it was only blobs of soybean paste, a few roasted nuts or a spoonful of cooked pumpkin leaves. As the famine continued, food prices across Malawi skyrocketed. There was less on the Kamkwamba table, and often William went to bed hungry. More and more of the family's meagre income went to buying food, leaving little for luxuries like kerosene to light lamps at night, or for books and school uniforms for William and his six sisters. By the end of the year, there was no money to send William to school. He was forced to drop out just a few weeks after starting grade nine.

"I decided I would build my own windmill."

Facing long, empty days, William looked for ways to keep occupied. He discovered a small library in Wimbe Primary School, one with three floor-to-ceiling shelves filled with books. William befriended the librarian and read in the shade outdoors, feasting on all kinds of subjects — Geography, Mathematics, Electronics.

One day William found a science book called *Using Energy*. The cover showed a long row of windmills. Inside, the pages described how windmills generated electricity and were used around the world to pump water and provide light.

To William, the book spelled hope. If a windmill could do

all of these things, imagine what one could do for his family. "Standing there looking at this book, I decided I would build my own windmill," he wrote later.

Each morning for a month, William headed to an abandoned scrapyard across from his former school. Machine parts littered the ground. Old pumps, springs, coils, pipes, sunbleached cars, rusty tractors — treasures for the taking.

William dragged pieces home and stashed them in his room, around his bed, behind the door — wherever he could find space. Guided by the textbook, he split some PVC pipe down the middle with a bow saw, heated it in a grass fire behind the kitchen to soften the plastic, hammered the pieces flat and shaped them into blades. He bolted four of the blades to a tractor fan and fastened the fan to the shaft of a giant shock absorber.

His father had a broken bicycle. It was missing handlebars, had only one wheel and the frame was rusty, but to William the wreck was perfect for his windmill — if only his father would give it to him.

William explained his plan, his dream of supplying the family with electricity, and water not only for drinking but perhaps better crops. "We could have lights! We could pump water and have an extra harvest. We'll never go hungry again!"

It took an hour of negotiating, but finally his father consented.

A local welder fastened the shock absorber to the bicycle frame. William's windmill was almost complete, but a crucial piece was still missing. To convert wind energy into electricity, he still needed a generator.

William reread the science book. Generators all work in much the same way. Magnets inside the generator turn, forcing electrical charges to flow through coils of insulated wire.

William searched the scrapyard for weeks looking for a

generator, but he came up empty-handed. Then one day as he and his friend Gilbert walked down a road, a stranger on a bicycle passed by. The man had a headlamp on the handlebars that was wired to a small generator rigged to his back tire. With each crank of the pedals, the tire spun, turning a small wheel on the generator, producing electricity to light the headlamp.

Knowing that William couldn't afford it on his own, Gilbert bought the generator for him. William connected it to his dad's bike frame. With the help of Gilbert and another friend, he built a 5-metre tower out of blue gum trees harvested from a nearby grove. Then, using wire borrowed from his mother's clothesline, William constructed a makeshift pulley system and hoisted the contraption to the top.

William's windmill atop a 5-metre-high tower.

Perched high above homes in the village, the windmill soon attracted curious visitors. Within minutes a dozen people had gathered at the base, eyes glued to the tower. Holding a light bulb connected by wires to the generator,

William stood with the crowd to watch and wonder along with the others: Would it work?

Wind whipped across the blades. They began to spin. The light bulb flickered, then glowed. The crowd cheered.

"It was glorious light . . . ! I threw my hands in the air and screamed with joy. I began to laugh so hard I became dizzy," William said.

He ran insulated copper wire from the windmill into the house, and connected the wire to light bulbs positioned in different rooms. There was no need to spend money on fuel for kerosene lamps now. Electricity was theirs and it was free, too.

But electricity was just one of the family's challenges. Their water supply came from a shallow well outside the house. Hauling water from the well one pail at a time was back-breaking work. Most days there was barely enough for drinking and washing clothes, leaving little for the parched crops.

In a book called *Explaining Physics*, William found a picture of a water pump. The pump didn't look too complicated — a system of pistons and valves that drew water through pipes. William figured he could make one.

At the scrapyard he found several plastic irrigation pipes. He fed a 12-metre section of pipe into the well, then inserted a thinner, metal pipe inside. Connected to a second windmill, the metal pipe moved up and down much like a piston, creating a vacuum that drew water out of the well. Over time William fine-tuned the device, greasing the sides, upgrading the tubes, perfecting his invention and adding improvements.

In an area often struck with drought, its people mostly poor, William's hand-built machines brought relief and independence. With an ample supply of electricity and water at their disposal, the Kamkwamba household prospered. There was money now for things like books and tuition fees. After a five-year absence, William returned to school. Encouraged by his teachers, he started a science club for students.

Word of William's success spread. Visitors drove long distances to take photographs of his "electric wind" machine. Reporters wrote about him in newspapers and magazines, and his story was featured on television and radio.

In 2007 William was invited to speak at a technology conference in Tanzania. Offers of scholarships to attend university followed, and he was invited to speak in far-off places. Inspired by William, people are building machines like his in other hard-struck areas of the world, bringing power and water to those most in need.

PEOPLE, HAVE SOME SHAME

Shocked by the desperate acts of fellow Egyptians, Asmaa Mahfouz boldly called for action.

The Egyptian woman in the YouTube video is small and slight. Wisps of black hair show beneath her *hijab* — her Muslim head covering. She looks younger than her twenty-six years and although she is speaking Arabic, you cannot shift your attention away. There is fire in her eyes, certainty in her voice, authority in her tone. When your eyes finally drift to the English translation that flows across the bottom of the screen, you catch a few words: *People, have some shame.*

During the almost thirty-year dictatorship of President Hosni

Mubarak, Egyptians like Asmaa Mahfouz, the woman in the video, lived in fear. Citizens had few human rights. It was even illegal to gather in groups of five or more without government approval. Beatings and torture were commonplace. Jails were filled with those who disobeyed the rules, those who spoke out about the corrupt police and Mubarak's strong-arm ways, or those who were even related to others who were presumed guilty. Fear of the government kept Egyptians quiet and oppressed.

Egyptian demonstrators took to the streets to call for the resignation of President Mubarak.

In April 2008 when workers in Mahalla, Egypt, protested their dire working conditions, Mahfouz took a bold step. Believing that change was necessary, she joined the Youth Movement. Along with hundreds of other student activists, she looked for ways to oust Mubarak and bring democracy to Egypt.

Like others in the Youth Movement, she operated secretly, wary of the police who had the power to arrest activists and imprison them without charges. The group criticized Mubarak's government and often used blogs and social networking sites like Facebook and Twitter to make their views known. Sometimes they posted YouTube videos that showed police beating and torturing citizens. Like others, Mahfouz kept her posts anonymous, never signing her name or showing her face, fearful of the harm that might come to her family and herself.

A young Tunisian street vendor set himself on fire to protest the unfair government.

On December 17, 2010, events in nearby Tunisia shocked the world. In an act known as self-immolation, a young street vendor named Mohamed Bouazizi set himself on fire to protest the unfair government. The act galvanized Tunisians. In solidarity, citizens rose as one, demonstrating and rioting in the streets. In the face of widespread opposition, the Tunisian president resigned.

In Egypt, four men followed Bouazizi's lead. In full public view, they set themselves on fire. One of the men, Ahmed Hashem el-Sayed, died. Shocked at the desperateness of their acts, Mahfouz made another video. But this one was different.

She sat in front of a camera in a stark room. Although her head was covered by a traditional *hijab*, her face was exposed. She identified herself and gave her Twitter account. Speaking Arabic in a clear, unwavering voice, she said: "Four Egyptians have set themselves on fire to protest humiliation and hunger and poverty and degradation they had to live with for thirty years . . . People, have some shame."

For four minutes and thirty-six seconds, the words rolled out, powerful and convincing. She talked about injustice and the abuse suffered by Egyptians under Mubarak. She talked about new possibilities for her country and the rights and responsibilities of each citizen. Finally she called on Egyptians to take action. "Sitting at home and just following us on the news or on Facebook leads to our humiliation — it leads to my humiliation . . . Go down to the street, send messages, post it on the Internet, make people aware."

She ended with a call for people to join together in protest at Cairo's Tahrir Square on January 25, 2011, a national holiday in Egypt. "We'll go and demand our rights, our fundamental human rights," she said.

The risks were high. Days before, she and other protesters had been arrested by police for speaking out against Mubarak. Now anyone who watched the video, even the police or Mubarak himself, would be able to identify her.

Within days the video went viral, shared around the world on cell phones and the Internet. Egyptians were struck by the boldness of Mahfouz's act. Encouraged by the reaction, she made other videos and repeated her call to action. On January 24, the day before the planned protest in Tahrir Square, she posted one more: "Tomorrow, if we make our stand despite all that security may do to us, and stand as one in peaceful protest, it will be the first real step on the road to change, the first real step that will take us forward."

On January 25 she went to Tahrir Square to protest, not knowing if police would arrest her, if she would be imprisoned or if her family would suffer consequences. She hoped she wouldn't be alone. To her surprise an estimated one million Egyptians joined her, filling the square and adjoining streets. Carrying signs and shouting slogans, they protested peacefully, demanding an end to the Mubarak regime.

United in their cause, Egyptians continued their non-violent protest over the following weeks. Overwhelmed by the opposition, Mubarak resigned on February 11, 2011.

Egypt still has hurdles to cross in its quest for fair and democratic government, but Asmaa Mahfouz's open challenge showed that in an age of social media, bold words can have greater influence than any other weapon.

FACING THE IMPOSSIBLE
June 16, 1976 / Soweto, South Africa

At a time when the Republic of South Africa was divided along racial lines, apartheid practices kept Blacks oppressed and segregated from Whites. In 1976 newspaper photographer Sam Nzima attended a protest rally of thousands of unarmed Black students in Soweto. Unexpectedly, the police opened fire, gunning down defenceless students at random. One was thirteen-year-old Hector Pieterson.

Nzima continued taking pictures, including one that showed Hector Pieterson's limp and lifeless body being carried by a fellow student. Knowing the police would want to confiscate the pictures and keep Soweto a secret from the rest of the world, Nzima removed the film from his camera, tucked it into his sock and then passed it on to his driver with instructions to take it to his office immediately.

The next day Nzima's photo of Hector Pieterson appeared in newspapers around the globe. Through that single picture, the world discovered the bloody truth about Soweto, beginning a wave of change that eventually saw an end to apartheid in South Africa.

"I was just shooting, I didn't have a sense of what pictures I was taking. . . . But something told me that I needed to protect these pictures," Sam Nzima told a reporter years later.

CREATING THE IMPOSSIBLE
September, 2007 / Cambridge, Nova Scotia, Canada

When grade-twelve students David Shepherd and Travis Price heard of a bullying incident at their school, they took action. A newcomer, a grade-nine boy, had worn a pink polo shirt on his first day. Bullies belittled the boy for his choice of clothing, calling him a homosexual and taunting him with names like *queer* and *fag*.

"I figured enough was enough," David said.

Deciding to show their support for the student in a unique way, David and Travis bought every pink T-shirt they could find at a nearby used-clothing store.

The two boys went online and e-mailed their classmates, offering them T-shirts and encouraging them to stand up to bullying by wearing pink the next day.

The reaction was overwhelming. The next morning the school was awash in a "sea of pink" as hundreds of students showed up wearing pink clothes.

The effect was twofold — the bullied boy felt the

support of his schoolmates, and the bullies knew their behaviour would not be tolerated.

News of the pink shirt episode spread, sparking an anti-bullying movement that continues to grow. Now, on the second Wednesday of each April, millions of people worldwide don pink clothes for International Pink Shirt Day, taking a stand against discrimination, much like David and Travis did at their school in 2007.

"We never expected this reaction," Travis said of the boys' idea and the results it achieved. "We did it simply because it felt right."

SWEPT INTO OBLIVION

Christopher was trapped waist-deep in sewage and breathing toxic air.

Fifteen-year-old Christopher Watt stood in waist-deep brown water, shivering from the cold. It was pitch black inside the sewer, and except for the gush of running water and his hollow cries for help, it was mostly quiet. The air was foul, reeking of human waste. Christopher's soggy clothes were caked with the disgusting stuff.

Hours before on that evening of June 10, 2000, Christopher had entered an open manhole at the corner of Walkley and Hawthorne roads in Ottawa, Ontario. With friends cheering him until the dare had gone wrong, he'd fallen off the slippery ladder and got caught in the swift flow. Carried by the current, he had rocketed down sewer lines and careened over spill-ways, moving ever closer to the Green Creek sewage treatment plant. He'd stopped before reaching the plant, though. Now he was standing inside a large concrete pipe, trapped somewhere in the city's 220-kilometre sewer system.

Each toxic breath was a reminder of the hopelessness of his situation. Survival seemed unlikely; rescue remote. *I'm going to die,* Christopher told himself.

* * *

Within minutes of his disappearance, Christopher's friends rallied. At 8:39 p.m. someone called 911 and started a chain reaction. Dozens of firefighters converged on the site. Soon they were joined by police, ambulance workers and mu-nicipal crews who understood the city's sewer system and its meandering ways. Minutes later Christopher's mother arrived.

Sewers carry their own special brand of danger. Decom-posing waste — the sludge tugging at Christopher's feet — removes oxygen from the air and replaces it with toxic gases like hydrogen sulphide, a substance even more dangerous than carbon monoxide. The first order of business for the firefighters was to test the air quality and measure oxygen levels. Then they determined what gear might be needed: self-contained breathing devices, tether ropes and other equipment that fit the rescue plan.

With testing complete, two firefighters climbed down the manhole, tethered by ropes and carrying portable air units. At the bottom they located an access tunnel and two hori-zontal sewer lines that joined into a single pipe. The pipe led to a small wall, then to an even smaller pipe no bigger than 40 centimetres in diameter.

Slippery sludge coated the sides of the pipe. There were no

handles to grab, no edges to stop the flow. They realized that once he'd been sucked into the system, Christopher must have gone for a terrifying ride, shooting into dark oblivion, unable to help himself.

This kid is not coming out alive.

The pipes led into the main trunk of the sewer system, a cavernous space filled with sewage and toxic air. Was Christopher even still alive?

Chief Wayne Brownlee, one of the firefighters on the scene, assessed Christopher's chances. "I figured we're not going to get this guy," he told a reporter from the *Ottawa Citizen*. Luc Dugal, the city's superintendent of sewer maintenance, agreed. "When I first heard that there was a kid down there, I thought: This kid is not coming out alive."

While firefighters followed the watery trail, a second rescue team climbed down another manhole at Sheffield Road, about 1800 metres from the one where Christopher had disappeared. The line was larger here, about 2.75 metres in diameter. The quick-thinking crew spread ladders across it, creating a makeshift "net." If Christopher shot this way, he would at least have something to grab, some way to stop himself.

Above ground, municipal workers scanned sewer maps, reading them by the interior lights of a van. The maps told them little that they didn't already know. If Christopher was in the main line, he would be standing in swiftly-flowing sewage, its temperature around 10° Celsius.

At 10:33 p.m. a call for help went out to Fire Station Number 2 on Preston Street, headquarters of a swift-water rescue team. The team had faced difficult situations before, usually in open water where victims required rescue from rivers, lakes or floodwaters. This situation was something quite different. Christopher, if he was alive, was trapped in total darkness somewhere underground, in a confined space — and possibly hundreds of metres from any access point the rescuers could use to reach him. Quite likely he was suffering from hypothermia, the enemy of clear thinking. The air he breathed would be a toxic mix.

"Stick your head in a toilet," one of the crew told the *Ottawa Citizen*. "That was what it was like."

The brown swill around Christopher carried harmful bacteria, too. He'd been immersed in the contaminants. Perhaps he'd even swallowed some. Who knew what infections they carried or dangers they posed to the swift-water rescue team.

Firefighters were dispatched to a spot about 600 metres from the maintenance cover where Christopher went down. The site was an access point, an entry into the main line. Factoring in curves and spillways, they decided that if the boy hadn't already been swept farther away, this was likely close to where he — or his body — might be found.

Two large, metal trap doors covered the shaft. Already maintenance workers had unlocked the doors and thrown them open. From deep below they heard a thin sound. A faraway voice — or so they thought. Was it Christopher calling for help?

Roughly twenty minutes later, four specially trained swiftwater rescuers from Fire Station Number 2 arrived, life jackets, helmets, waterproof radios and other gear in tow. They carried an oddly shaped inflatable boat called a Rapid Deployment Craft, designed for water-rescue operations. Large enough for two paddlers, it has a flat base that opens at each end into a large loop. The open-end design allows rescuers to position themselves directly over the heads and shoulders of victims trapped in water — an advantage when pulling them aboard.

The swift-water rescuers had used the craft before on open water sites. But below ground, in a dark sewer slippery with sludge and reeking of toxic gases? This would be the ultimate test of their skills.

The Rapid Deployment Craft's looped ends allow rescuers to get very close to victims.

Dean Taylor and Barry Blondin, two of the swift-water rescuers, quickly pulled on their gear. Other rescuers rigged an improvised pulley system to the top of the shaft so the craft could be lowered into the water. They worked carefully, aware that the ropes might fray and break when rubbed against the rough concrete. To lose the vessel to the churning water now would cost precious minutes . . . and possibly Christopher's life.

At 11:29 p.m., tethered by ropes to secure it, the boat hit the water. Wearing breathing devices, wetsuits and special footgear,

Taylor and Blondin climbed aboard. A 100-metre rope tied to the craft led to rescuers stationed above. The rope was a lifeline, a precaution should the current be too strong or if the men encountered trouble and needed to be reeled back.

Taylor and Blondin paddled through the foul water, pointing two powerful headlamps ahead to light up the tunnel. The water flowed far faster than they expected, and in no time the rope reached its end. Another section of rope was knotted onto the first by the crew above. Then a third. A fourth.

They called Christopher's name. Above the spill of water, they heard a muffled reply. "We're coming," the men called. "We're coming."

The main line curved and followed a steady downward slope. Deep below the surface, their two-way radios stopped working. Normally this would end a rescue attempt. If the men were unable to communicate with crews above, it would be too dangerous to continue this way. But Taylor and Blondin had a backup plan. They carried whistles attached to their life jackets. Blowing sharply in short bursts, they sent messages to the others above. *We're all right. Keep paying out the rope.*

The lights scanned the concrete pipe, offering shadowy glimpses ahead. Around midnight a figure appeared out of the dark — Christopher was up ahead.

At almost the same time, the rope tightened. The craft stopped. Just 15 metres from Christopher, the rope paid out and fell short of its target. Six ropes knotted together by now . . . and still another was needed. The surface crew tied on a seventh, then released the rope, paying it out gradually. When the craft reached Christopher, Taylor and Blondin blew a signal to stop. Positioning the open end of the boat over the boy, Taylor hauled him aboard. Then he strapped a life jacket on Christopher and secured him with rope to the rescue craft.

Christopher amid the rescuers who managed to reach him.

"He said he thought he was going to die," Taylor reported. "He said it four or five times."

The men signalled the crew above to begin hauling them back. Somehow the crew missed the signal. Taylor jumped into the water. While he pushed the Rapid Deployment Craft upstream, Blondin stayed on the boat and pulled the rope to reel it in and coil it on the floor. When it proved difficult, he asked Christopher to help.

Forty-one minutes after Taylor and Blondin had entered the sewer line, they were back at the starting point, their mission finally accomplished. Weak and shivering, Christopher climbed up the shaft.

Because he had been submerged in sewage, a hazardous waste unit skilled in decontamination took over. Christopher was hosed down with antibacterial solution, given a pair of emergency overalls and then shuttled to hospital for tests and observation. Given a clean bill of health, he was released a few days later, none the worse for his misadventure, but wiser from the experience.

News of his rescue circulated quickly. It could have turned out much worse, experts agreed. That evening the sewer's main line had been only partly full. Had it been raining, had the sewers been running at maximum capacity, had the Rapid Deployment Craft not worked as planned, Christopher would have drowned.

SURVIVING THE IMPOSSIBLE
November 2011 / Western Australia

When flames from a raging bushfire neared his home, Peter Fabrici did what he could to save his house. He donned non-combustible clothes and doused himself with water. Then he put sprinklers on the roof and stuffed rags into the downspouts to flood the eavestroughs with runoff.

Temperatures rose. The air filled with thick smoke. Wearing goggles and breathing oxygen through a mouthpiece rigged to a scuba tank on a small, wheeled trolley, Fabrici fought on. When the situation worsened, he was forced to retreat. Goggles on, mouthpiece in place, scuba gear by his side, he leaped into his neighbour's pool and plunged to the bottom.

Fabrici's quick-thinking action paid off. "It all worked beautifully." he said. "The house is still there and I'm still alive."

FLYING LIKE SUPERMAN

In a panic, the lost boy searched the train, screaming his brother's name.

Saroo Munshi Khan's past haunted him. In dreams or in quiet moments, images from more than twenty years earlier floated into his head — a bridge, a train station, a dam overflowing with water. He saw himself as a young boy, running down dusty streets, over train tracks, to a mud hut that looked familiar. A family lived there — his family. Occasionally Saroo saw their faces . . . his mother . . . his brothers . . . his sister.

Much of Saroo's past was a mystery. When he was five years old, he lived in India in a tiny mud hut with a tin roof. His family was poor. His father had abandoned them, and his mother, Kamala, spent most days hauling bricks and cement at construction sites.

Saroo was especially close to his nine-year-old brother, Guddu. Often Guddu took Saroo with him when he searched for fallen coins at the train station or gathered scraps of meat in the market or raided chicken coops for eggs.

Saroo couldn't read or write. He didn't know the name of his town or even his own surname, but he had a gift — a keen sense of direction. As they walked, Saroo kept track of familiar markers — a fountain on the left, a bridge on the right, a turn in the road ahead. If he became separated from Guddu, Saroo followed the mental map he had created, sometimes even beating his brother home.

One evening Guddu took Saroo to the train station to hunt for coins. They boarded a train bound for Burhanpur, a town two hours away, combing the floorboards for coins passengers had dropped. By the time the train arrived at Burhanpur, Saroo was exhausted. While they waited for the next train back, he rested on a bench.

"Stay here. Don't go anywhere," Guddu told him. "I'll be back for you."

Saroo fell asleep. When he woke up, it was dark and Guddu was nowhere to be seen. Groggily, Saroo boarded a train, figuring that his brother would be waiting inside. Again he fell into a deep sleep. When he awoke this time, it was morning. In panic he searched the train, screaming Guddu's name, looking for the brother who wasn't there.

At the next stop, Saroo left the train and wandered the station. It was a large and foreign place filled with strangers who spoke languages different from Saroo's Hindi. He couldn't read the signs, and when he asked for help no one understood him. Lost and far from home, he had no food, no money and no idea of just how far he had gone or the route he had taken. Bewildered and afraid, he scrambled aboard another train, hoping it would take him home. Instead he ended up at an even larger and busier station. Although he didn't know it then, Saroo had reached Calcutta, the capital of the Indian province of West Bengal.

Calcutta's busy streets are thronged with people and traffic.

Over the next few days Saroo rode trains in and out of Calcutta, desperately looking for one that would return him to his family. Finally he gave up. For a time the Calcutta train station, then the city's slums, became his home. To survive, Saroo scrounged for food in trash cans or begged strangers for handouts. He slept in alleyways, curled up against buildings, homeless like so many others in Calcutta.

Could he find his way home? he wondered.

Thanks to a kind man who spoke a little Hindi, Saroo ended up under the care of the Indian Society for Sponsorship and Adoption (ISSA), a non-profit child-welfare group. He was adopted by an Australian couple who lived in Hobart, Tasmania. Even though the adjustment was difficult, Saroo fell into a new life there. He was given a new last name: Brierley. Sheltered and loved by his adoptive parents, he learned Australian ways. He was popular, excelled at sports and achieved decent grades at school. Eventually he went to college, moved into his own apartment and worked on the website of a company owned by his adoptive parents.

Fleeting glimpses from his past still appeared, however. Certain memories seemed especially vivid. The day wild dogs had chased him and he tripped, gashing his forehead on a rock, for example. Or the time he had cut his leg while climbing a fence near a fountain. And then there were dreams — the mud hut that had once been home, the family that had once been his.

Saroo filled the emptiness he sometimes felt with other things — work, parties, long hours on the Internet. Then in 2009, after a breakup with a girlfriend, memories came flooding back. He felt a need to know more about himself and his Indian family.

Saroo launched Google Earth on his laptop, using its satellite imagery and aerial photography to give overhead views of cities and streets. In minutes he was "zooming" over India — flying, as he put it, "just like Superman." Could he find his home this way? he wondered.

India is a large, heavily populated country dotted with numerous cities and villages. Saroo didn't know his town's name, nor did he remember any of the Hindi he once spoke. He hadn't been able to read when he was five years old, so when he tried to find the town where he had become separated from Guddu, there seemed to be countless choices that sounded or looked like the name he vaguely remembered. Many of the names were spelled in similar ways and sounded almost the same.

The Calcutta train station seemed a logical choice to begin. It had been his end point, the final stop of his journey. By working backward and retracing his route from there, Saroo thought he might find his starting point — the town where he once lived. Using Google Earth he zipped along the tracks, following them as they criss-crossed the country, into one town, out to the next.

Saroo continued his Google Earth search on and off for three years. With only a few leads to follow and so many routes available, locating his home seemed impossible. He found himself going over the same tracks again and again. There had to be a better way, but what was it?

One night in 2012 it came to him. Drawing on his memories, Saroo revisited the evening he had become separated from Guddu. He'd fallen asleep on the train. The next morning he had woken up in Calcutta. About twelve hours had elapsed. If he could find out how fast the train had been going, he could calculate how far it had travelled and narrow his search.

He contacted four Indian friends on Facebook and Myspace and asked if they could find out from their parents how fast trains travelled in India in the 1980s. By averaging their answers, Saroo arrived at a speed of 80 kilometres an hour. He multiplied that by twelve hours. His answer — the train had travelled about 960 kilometres.

On a Google Earth satellite image, he drew a circle with Calcutta at the centre and a radius of 960 kilometres. That circle defined his search area. Still, it was a large space with numerous possibilities. Was there a way of narrowing it down even more?

India is a complex country with many climate zones, cultures and languages. Saroo had been told that his facial structure resembled people who came from East India, so he concentrated his search on that portion of the circle. He also realized that he could eliminate places where Hindi wasn't spoken and where the climate was different from what he remembered.

With the scope of the hunt narrowed, Saroo followed the tracks leading out of the Calcutta station, "flying" over them with Google Earth. He looked for markers from his youth, like the fountain where he once gashed his leg or the cafe he often passed on his way into town.

Late one night, after months of investigation, Saroo spotted a hazy image of a bridge. The bridge was next to a train station. The scene looked familiar. He zoomed closer. There was a sign posted on the station. *Burhanpur* — the place where he'd become separated from his brother — and a name he only vaguely knew.

"I had a shock," Saroo said. This was it, the station where he and Guddu had lost one another. Home was just hours away.

Saroo flew along the tracks, skimming over trees and rooftops with Google Earth. He stopped at another station. There was a dam nearby with a river that flowed over it like a waterfall. It too seemed familiar.

Drawing on the mental map from his youth, Saroo moved the cursor away from the station and used it to travel the nearby streets. After a number of turns he seemed able to remember, he arrived at the centre of town, at the fountain where he'd scarred his leg climbing a fence all those years ago.

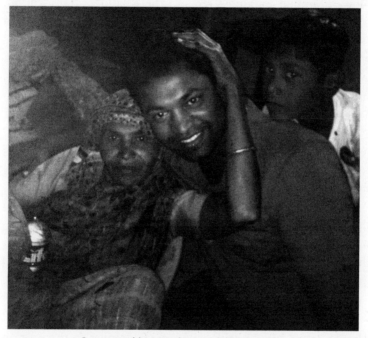

Saroo and his mother at their reunion.

The town's name was Khandwa. Despite all of the familiar markers, Saroo still had doubts. Was this really the right place?

On Facebook he found a group called *Khandwa My Home Town*. "Can anyone help me?" he asked.

Saroo described the features he remembered from his youth. He mentioned that he vaguely recalled living in a suburb outside the main town, in a region that was predominately Hindu.

"Can anyone tell me the name of this neighbourhood . . . I think it starts with a G."

The answer came a few days later: Ganesh Talai.

On February 10, 2012, Saroo boarded an airplane and flew to the airport closest to Khandwa. He hopped a taxi and followed familiar looking streets to the Khandwa train station. He was positive this was where he had been with Guddu twenty-five years ago on their last evening together.

Saroo stood for a while on the platform, awash in memories. Then he walked down busy streets, past spots he had charted on his mental map, past places he had pictured in his dreams. Eventually he found himself in front of a tiny mud hut with a tin roof.

A woman emerged from the house. "Do you need help?" she asked. Saroo pulled out a photograph his adoptive parents had taken of him when he was a boy. "Do you know where my family is?" he asked.

Although his family no longer lived there, a neighbour led him to another house not far away. Three women wearing colourful saris stood outside. The one in the middle was older than the others. Without saying anything, the woman stepped forward. It was his mother, Kamala. She hugged Saroo, took him by the hand and welcomed him home.

"How do you know this is your son?" some of the neighbours asked her. In reply, she simply pointed to the scar on Saroo's forehead, proof of his encounter with wild dogs all those years ago.

News spread of the lost son who had come home. Soon other members of the family gathered at the house, eager to reconnect with Saroo. One person was absent, though. "Where is Guddu?" Saroo asked.

Kamala told the story of the day Saroo had disappeared. Guddu hadn't come home either, it turned out. His body was later discovered on the train tracks. For Kamala, it was a double blow. One son was dead; the other missing. Her heart was broken, and life was never quite the same afterward.

For Saroo, the journey he'd started with Google Earth was complete. Although Tasmania was now his home, he had roots in India, too. The family of his youth was there; the gaps in his past were filled. Before he flew back to Tasmania, Saroo swore a solemn promise. He would keep the ties in Khandwa alive, he told his mother, no matter how far away he lived.

OVERCOMING THE IMPOSSIBLE
April 1, 2009 / Oxford, England

When a teen in Maryland, US, received a message that an English boy she had befriended on Facebook was planning on killing himself, she told her mother. Little was known about the boy — just his last name and the school he attended in Oxford — but the girl's mother notified Maryland Police. From there the message passed to the White House, then to the British Embassy in Washington, then to the Metropolitan Police in London and finally to Thames Valley Police who patrolled the district where the school was located, 5000 kilometres away from Maryland.

After searching on Google and checking voting lists for a match to the boy's last name, the local police narrowed their list of potential addresses to eight locations in Oxford. At one home after the other they knocked on doors, asking residents if a teen in trouble lived there. At the third address, police found the teen unconscious in his upstairs bedroom, suffering from a drug overdose. His parents, downstairs at the time, were unaware of the problem. The boy was rushed to hospital, where he made a full recovery.

From the time the teen had posted his Facebook comment to the moment he was discovered, only two-and-a-half hours had passed. "It was a race against time," Sergeant Paul Sexton, Acting Inspector for Oxford that night, said. "We didn't know what we were going to find. He could have been dead. I was so happy when I heard he had been found safe."

126 DAYS IN HELL

With their eyes trained on the street, the rebels didn't notice the rescue plan unfolding below their feet.

Just before the explosion, Canadian Ambassador Anthony Vincent had been chatting with other diplomats. His wife, Lucie, was outside on the garden patio. It was December 17, 1996, Japanese Emperor Akihito's birthday, a reason to celebrate. At the Japanese ambassador's residence in Lima, Peru, waiters served sushi and opened champagne bottles as the Vincents and five hundred other guests mingled, their cares mostly forgotten.

At 8:20 p.m. a powerful blast rattled glasses and ended

conversations. Seconds later fourteen armed rebels dressed all in black crashed the party. Some entered through a hole blown through the garden wall. Others disguised as waiters pulled out automatic weapons hidden in large flower arrangements.

"This is the Tupac Amaru Revolutionary Movement," one of them announced. "Obey, and nothing will happen to you."

"We'll shoot you if you move or say anything."

Warning shots were fired into the air, followed by shouts and orders. "Don't look at us. Down on the ground. We'll shoot you if you move or say anything." Ambassador Vincent and his wife obeyed. So did other terrified guests.

Outside, police reacted swiftly. They lobbed tear gas canisters into the compound and fired bullets. The rebels pulled on gas masks they had brought and fired back. After forty minutes one of the rebels forced a megaphone into the Japanese ambassador's hand.

"Get up," he ordered.

Repeating the words dictated by the rebel, the ambassador called out to police: "Please respect the integrity of my guests and stop shooting. You're going to kill them."

The shooting stopped. The rebels herded hostages, hands above their heads, into the mansion. "Sit on the floor," they ordered. "Be quiet. Don't do anything stupid."

Doors were closed, windows sealed and curtains drawn. Stationing themselves around the mansion, the rebels held the hostages at gunpoint.

The rebels' motives soon became clear. Led by Nestor Cerpa, they demanded the release of 450 Tupac Maru prisoners in exchange for the hostages' lives. The rebels had been active in Peru for years. Wanting to bring down the Peruvian government and establish a communist-style one in its place, the Tupac Maru had launched bloody attacks — bombings, hijackings, kidnappings, slayings of key officials. In response, the government, led by President Alberto Fujimori, had outlawed the group, hunted down supporters and jailed thousands of suspected Tupac Maru sympathizers.

The rebels who had stormed the residence that evening would do anything for Nestor Cerpa, even die if necessary.

* * *

Around midnight, the rebels released some of the older hostages and all of the women, including Lucie Vincent. Hours later they released a few others. Ambassador Vincent was in this group, released early because he volunteered to act as a negotiator for the rebels.

In the days that followed, other hostages were released. Just before Christmas, in an act of goodwill, Cerpa freed 225 more. Finally just 72 hostages remained. One was President Fujimori's brother Pedro. To Cerpa and his followers these were the most important hostages — dignitaries with influence who provided the greatest bargaining power.

To oversee discussions and mediate terms, President Fujimori appointed a commission of "guarantors." Ambassador Vincent was one, chosen because he was trusted by rebels and government alike. As the standoff dragged on, the ambassador shuttled in and out of the Japanese residence, relaying news, settling nerves and encouraging a peaceful settlement. When asked why he risked his life each time going back, he answered simply, "Because I gave my word."

On the surface, President Fujimori seemed willing to negotiate. In secret, however, he had other plans. Weeks before, he had visited an ancient temple at the Chavin de Huantar site in northern Peru. The temple was a maze of interconnecting passageways. In its construction, Fujimori saw promise — a solution to the rebel problem and a way to free the hostages.

Borrowing ideas from the Chavin de Huantar site, President Fujimori ordered the military to construct a series of tunnels linking houses in the embassy neighbourhood with main points under the Japanese residence. Thirty miners from northern Peru were brought to Lima. Working rotating four-hour shifts, the miners chipped and carved the rock, working as quietly as possible as they dug five tunnels — one main and four branches, each about 3 metres below ground.

The miners braced the main tunnel with steel and heavy timber, equipped it with electric lights and padded the floor with carpet to deaden sounds. They stocked it with food and weapons. Wide enough for two men to stand side by side, it was also tall enough for an average-sized person to walk upright.

The rebels who had stormed the residence that evening would do anything, even die.

At the same time, on the street in front of the Japanese residence, a carefully orchestrated distraction unfolded. Military vehicles circled the grounds, spinning wheels and grinding gears while helicopters chopped overhead. Soldiers ran through noisy training manoeuvres and a police band played loud marches, pounding drums and blasting horns.

To the rebels inside the residence, the round-the-clock noise was unsettling. It disturbed their sleep and rattled their nerves. It left them wondering, too. Just what was going on out there? With their eyes trained on the street, with the loud noise swallowing other sounds, the rebels didn't notice the rescue plan unfolding below their feet.

One day in mid-January a surprise package arrived at the Japanese residence. It was a gift for the hostages, a new guitar to replace another one that the rebels had claimed for themselves. Embedded inside was a tiny electronic microphone and battery unit, the perfect listening device.

Using planted video and sound equipment, the military eavesdropped on the rebels and collected key information — what weapons the rebels carried, the patterns of their movements, the location of hostages throughout the house. The devices also allowed them to secretly transmit important messages to the men trapped inside.

Meanwhile in a port city not far from Lima, construction started on a mock-up of the Japanese ambassador's residence. One hundred and forty commandos, hand-picked from Peru's navy, army and air force, were sent to the site. They experimented with manoeuvres in the copy-cat mansion — running down fake corridors, bursting through doors, seizing control from the rebels. They rehearsed their moves, knowing that in a real rescue every second counted. By their calculations, fifty per cent of the hostages might be casualties if Operation Chavin de Huantar, as the plan was called, took more than a few minutes.

* * *

Inside the residence, tensions mounted. Most mornings the rebels ran drills, screaming threats at the hostages and holding guns to their heads as they practised repelling attacks. Sometimes the rebels pretended to lob grenades at the captives, increasing fears of huge casualties if ever there was a rescue attempt.

As months wore on, rebels and hostages both grew discouraged. Negotiations stalled. Through it all, Ambassador Vincent and the other guarantors continued their visits, hoping to negotiate peaceful terms.

Using planted video and sound equipment, the military eavesdropped on the rebels.

To ease tensions, some of the rebels played indoor soccer. Other rebels watched or took short naps. The game soon became a daily ritual, a refreshing break in the otherwise dull routine.

Occasionally, when there were breaks in the game and the residence grew quiet, muffled sounds could be heard below the floor. In March, when Ambassador Vincent made one of his frequent visits, Cerpa called him into the dining room.

"Put your ear to the floor," Cerpa said. "They are digging tunnels, aren't they?"

Vincent said nothing and hid his surprise. He hadn't been informed about Operation Chavin de Huantar. As much as he wanted the standoff to end peacefully, Vincent realized that the outcome was largely out of his hands.

* * *

By mid-April the tunnels were finished, the commandos were ready and the military knew the habits of those inside the house. Plastic explosives had been planted in the main tunnel, right under the floor of the residence. With the rebels' permission, clean clothes were delivered to the hostages. Instead of dark-coloured outfits like those the rebels wore, the hostages dressed in light-coloured clothing. Against the backdrop of dark rebel clothes, the hostages looked like pale ghosts, easily distinguishing them from the Tupac Maru.

Using a hidden two-way radio, the military transmitted a warning to one of the hostages, a Peruvian naval officer. When the commandos were ready, the Peruvian navy anthem would be played outside two days in a row. An assault would follow.

On Monday, April 21, 1997, small groups of commandos disguised as police entered houses surrounding the residence. They descended into the tunnels, traded their police uniforms for camouflage and waited for morning. At sunrise the commandos donned helmets and bulletproof vests. They checked weapons and explosives. They reviewed the plans. Then they waited some more.

Above ground, for the second day in a row, loudspeakers blasted the anthem. *We're coming*, the coded message said to the hostages. *Take cover.*

Through microphones planted around the residence, intelligence officers tracked the rebels' movements. They listened for familiar sounds — the shuffle of feet, the shouts and cheers of opposing teams. Would the rebels play soccer like they had so many other afternoons?

Just after 3:00 p.m. the Peruvian naval officer issued a report on his secret transmitter. The soccer game was on. All fourteen rebels were either playing the game, watching it or distracted with other duties.

It's a go, the naval officer was told. Calmly the officer spread the news to the other hostages. Lying flat on the bedroom floors, the men shielded their faces. If the assault took too long or if something went wrong, they would be likely targets.

Around 3:15 p.m. a goal was scored. At the same moment

commandos blew a hole in the floor. Tear gas launched through windows filled the rooms with smoke. From the hole, thirty commandos emerged, gas masks over their faces, automatic weapons ready. Twenty more commandos stormed the front door and chased fleeing rebels, aiming to stop them before they reached the hostages on the second floor.

A Peruvian soldier gets ready to storm the residence of the Japanese ambassador.

While helicopters circled, snipers stationed on roofs of neighbouring buildings opened fire. More commandos poured from side tunnels that opened in the backyard. They scaled ladders that had been placed against the rear walls of the residence, blew out a door on the second floor and blasted two holes in the roof. Through billowing black smoke, the commandos led hostages down an outside stairway to safety.

The assault was televised live. After 126 days, it was over in just 20 minutes. All 14 rebels were killed. Two commandos died, one while opening the balcony door to reach the hostages, another as he led them away. Of the 72 hostages, all made it out of the building alive, although one later died of a heart attack.

Peruvian President Alberto Fujimori walks through one of the tunnels two days after the dramatic rescue took place.

Across the country, Peruvians celebrated the success of Operation Chavin de Huantar. To this day, though, the mission is steeped in controversy. Arguments rage that rebels were killed unnecessarily, that some were shot while trying to surrender and that a peaceful settlement might have been possible with more time and effort. Others justify the method, saying it was the only option.

LIFE OR DEATH – ESCAPE

THIS SIDE UP WITH CARE

The wooden box looked ordinary enough. No one suspected there was a man inside.

August 1848. Richmond, Virginia: Three hundred and fifty Black slaves were being led down a street. Men, women and teenagers marched forward, ropes tied around their necks, their arms and hands bound, while young children rode in wagons. Many of the slaves were in tears. Sold to a new owner in North Carolina, they knew they would probably never see their families again . . .

Henry Brown, himself a slave who belonged to a different owner, stood on the street watching as his three children and his wife, Nancy, who was pregnant with their fourth child, were sold away. There was no chance for him to say goodbye, no opportunity to hug his children one last time.

That heartbreaking moment, the sight of his family being

led away while he stood powerless to prevent it, stayed with Brown. *I cannot express, in language, what were my feelings on this occasion,* he would write later.

At slave auctions it was common for people to be sold away from their families.

From that point on, Brown was a changed person. He vowed that whatever it took, he would find a way to escape slavery and become a free man.

The next year he contacted James Anthony Smith, a free Black man and friend. When Brown asked for his support, Smith put him in touch with a White storekeeper named Samuel Alexander Smith, a man who had helped other slaves gain their freedom.

"I told him I had a little money," Brown said, "and if he would assist me I would pay him for so doing."

It was a risky step for both men. If Brown was caught escaping, the penalties could be severe — punishment for himself, but also for the men who were helping him. Even so, they struck a deal and settled upon a price. For $86 — half of the money Brown had managed to save — Samuel Smith agreed to help him escape.

The men discussed escape plans that had been used before. None of them suited Brown or his situation. Then one day a solution appeared. "I was at work," he later explained, "when the idea suddenly flashed across my mind of shutting myself up in a box and getting myself conveyed as dry goods to a free state."

The idea was deceptively simple. Construct a large wooden box. Hide inside. Ship the box to Philadelphia, Pennsylvania, where slavery was outlawed. If he survived the trip, when the box was opened he would be a free man.

Samuel Smith contacted James Miller McKim, a leader of the Philadelphia Vigilance Committee, an anti-slavery group. Would he accept shipment of such a box when it arrived? Assured that he would, Brown designed a wooden box for the journey. It was 0.6 metres wide, 1 metre long and 0.8 metres deep. A bladder of water was tucked inside, along with a few biscuits. To provide air, three holes were drilled through the wood.

On March 23, 1849, Henry Brown squeezed his ample frame into the crate. He was 1.75-metres tall and weighed close to 90 kilograms. To fit, he folded his body and wedged it inside the box with his face pressed against the ventilation holes. The two Smiths nailed the box shut and looped five hickory hoops around to make sure it stayed sealed. Stamped on the box was the message: *This side up with care.*

Addressed to James Miller McKim in Philadelphia, the box began a complicated journey. Many times it was loaded and unloaded, moved from wagon to railroad car, to the deck of a steamboat, then to another wagon, another railroad car, a ferry, yet another wagon. The box was handled roughly and the message on the outside was often ignored. Sometimes the box was even carried upside down.

Brown suffered bumps and bruises, but was careful not to utter a sound. Despite the ventilation holes, the air grew stale and stifling. Driven by his quest, Brown kept his goal in mind. He resolved "to conquer or die trying."

The steamboat leg of the journey proved to be the most difficult. The box was stood on end with Brown upside down. For several hours he endured the painful position. "I felt my eyes swelling as if they would burst from their sockets and the veins on my temples were dreadfully distended with pressure of blood upon my head."

On the point of passing out, he heard the voices of two workmen outside. One complained about standing too long. He needed a place to sit. Suddenly Brown felt the box tilt. It slammed hard on the deck, right side up again. The wood creaked as the two men sat down and rested their tired legs. "I was relieved from a state of agony which may be more easily imagined than described," he said.

After twenty-seven hours, the box finally arrived at the office of the Pennsylvania Anti-Slavery Society in Philadelphia. James McKim was there along with several other members of the abolitionist movement. No sound came from inside the box. Was Henry Brown still alive?

McKim rapped on the lid. "All right?" he called.

"All right, sir!" Brown answered.

With saws and hatchets, the hoops were cut, the lid was raised and a wobbly Henry Brown rose up from the box, alive and free. "How do you do, gentlemen?" he said, reaching out his hand.

Brown's incredible journey in the small box ended in Philadelphia.

News of Henry "Box" Brown's bold escape captured the imagination of many. He became active in the Anti-Slavery Society, published a book about his adventures and travelled extensively, giving speeches about his experience.

In 2001 a metal replica of the famous box was installed at Canal Walk in downtown Richmond, Virginia, at a place where many slaves were bought and sold before the practice was finally outlawed in 1865.

OVERCOMING THE IMPOSSIBLE
August–October 1931 / Australia

During the first half of the twentieth century, with integration into White society the goal, Australian, Canadian and other governments ordered the widespread removal of aboriginal children from their homes. The children were shipped to state-run institutions and schools, sometimes many kilometres away. There they were stripped of their identities, denied access to their culture and forced to learn new languages and ways. Often they endured punishment and abuse.

Among the thousands plucked from their homes were three mixed-race girls living in Western Australia: Molly Craig, fourteen; her half-sister, Daisy Kadibil, eleven; and their cousin Gracie Fields, eight. Immediately after being shipped to the Moore River Settlement, 1600 kilometres from their home in Jigalong, Molly began to plot their escape.

On their second day the three girls hid in the dormitory and then walked out unnoticed. Carrying little food or clothing, wearing no shoes, they headed for home. To find their way they followed the Rabbit-Proof Fence — designed to stop the spread of rabbits — which ran north to south across Western Australia.

Eager to reach their families, the girls crossed the wilderness, walking up to 32 kilometres a day. At the start, rains washed away their footprints, helping them elude search parties. They approached farmhouses to ask for help, and ate whatever they could forage or catch: *bibijali* or sweet potato, pried out of the earth; *karkula*, a type of wild banana, harvested from trees; even rabbits, snared and cooked over an open fire. At night the three slept in rabbit burrows or on the ground, curled among sand dunes and scrub grass. When the younger girls grew tired and their legs became infected by grass cuts, Molly carried them.

A few weeks into their journey, Gracie learned from a woman they met that her mother had moved from Jigalong. Too exhausted to travel farther on foot, she hopped a train. Molly and Daisy continued their journey. After a trek lasting two months, the two girls reached Jigalong.

Protected by their parents, the girls stayed hidden and dodged authorities for a few more weeks until the search for them was finally abandoned, bringing an end to their remarkable ordeal.

VAULTING TO FREEDOM

Lulled by the predictable routine, the German guards never suspected that an escape was underway.

During World War II, escape was a priority at Stalag Luft III, a German prisoner-of-war camp in Poland. Most of the POWs were Allied airmen who had been shot down and captured. To tunnel out of the camp, to escape and return home to fly into battle once more — this was the duty and the dream of many prisoners, including Eric Williams and Richard Codner, two British airmen.

Unfortunately there was no easy way out of Stalag Luft III. The remote camp was a fortress, guarded by sentries in high wooden towers and surrounded by double 4-metre-high fences. The soil around the camp was loose and unstable and more sand than clay. Escape tunnels dug from the prisoner barracks at the centre of camp, 46 metres from the outer fences, often collapsed. To further complicate things, while the topsoil was dark grey, the subsoil was bright yellow — a colour easily detected. Several tunnel diggers had been caught when traces of yellow soil had been found on their shoes and clothes.

Those caught trying to escape faced harsh penalties. Sometimes the entire camp would be punished. To boost the chances of success and to minimize risk, the POWs established a secret escape committee. The committee studied escape plans, approved only those that seemed likely to succeed and gave their full support to those that passed inspection.

Eric Williams and Richard Codner analyzed the earlier unsuccessful attempts. Other tunnels had failed, they figured, because they started at the barracks, too far from the barbed wire fences. Furthermore, the tunnels had been dug mostly at night when guards were on alert for escapes and when seismograph microphones planted in the ground were active. A shovel chewing through the dirt, a foot running along the ground — the slightest vibration brought out guards and snarling attack dogs.

Why not start the tunnel closer to the fences? Williams and Codner suggested. Dig by day when the guards least expected it. Do it in the open, right under the guards' noses, but use a clever disguise to conceal the diggers.

The idea seemed too wild and extreme to work. But then there was a chance, too, a sliver of hope that it might succeed. The escape committee approved the plan and vowed to help the two men achieve their freedom.

To start, Eric Williams and Richard Codner oversaw the

construction of a wooden vaulting horse, the kind used by gymnasts to spring into the air. For building materials, the two men removed wooden rafters from an abandoned bathhouse inside the camp. The rafters became the vaulting horse's framework. To make the horse sturdy but also hollow and lightweight, they covered the frame with plywood rescued from Red Cross cartons. Two long shafts inserted through the horse became handles for four men to carry it. When completed, the horse stood 1.4 metres high and had a base 1.6 metres by 1 metre.

With the approval of the German guards, the POWs started an exercise routine. Each afternoon they carried the empty vaulting horse to an open field between the barracks and the barbed wire fences. It was placed on the ground — in exactly the same spot each time — between two pits, the jumping and landing places for the vaulters. While the guards watched, prisoners lined up and carried out a drill . . . running . . . vaulting over the horse . . . landing with a thud. Sometimes one of the vaulters purposely stumbled, knocking the horse over to show the guards that it was empty. Lulled by the predictable routine, the guards relaxed. On the afternoon of July 8, 1943, when the vaulting horse was carried out again, it was just another day for them — nothing to worry about, just POWs exercising as usual.

That day Codner was inside, bracing himself against the framework of the horse as it was carried. In his arms, he balanced a box containing a few digging supplies. The horse was placed on the ground in the usual spot. The shafts were withdrawn. Fresh air wafted through the holes at either end. As the prisoners vaulted, Codner began digging a tunnel while hiding beneath the vaulting horse. Two hours later, when the exercise period was over, he hid inside the vaulting horse again as it was carried to the barracks.

After that Williams and Codner took turns, or sometimes went together. Their tools were simple: trowels, wooden bowls, crude spades fashioned from tin cans. Working in stifling heat, they dug and scraped. They shovelled the dirt into small bags made from pant legs sewn together by the escape committee. When the vaulting horse was carried back to the barracks, the bags of dirt went with it.

A third man — Oliver Philpot, a Canadian pilot — worked mostly behind the scenes. In exchange for his help, Williams and Codner promised Philpot a chance at freedom, too. Philpot organized the vaulters, made sure materials were ready and transferred the sacks of sand. Other POWs hid the sacks in their pants. As they roamed the camp, they released little bits of sand, burying some under the barracks and digging some into the garden.

To prevent collapse, the shaft entrance was reinforced with bricks and bed boards smuggled out of the barracks. A wooden trap door set half a metre below the surface and covered with grey topsoil hid the opening and muffled hollow sounds the German guards might hear if they walked over it.

They were still 18 metres from the fence.

To light their way, Williams and Codner used candles. With little circulation in the cramped space, the air grew stale and unbearably warm. Often they stripped down to their waists or even worked naked, not only to combat the heat, but also to prevent the yellow sand from sticking to their clothes and giving them away.

There were close calls. Once, while Codner was tunnelling, part of the roof gave way. A hole appeared in the ground above. To hide the spot, a quick-thinking prisoner leaped over the vaulting horse, pretended to trip and landed over the opening. He faked a twisted leg and moaned in agony, stalling the exercise routine and buying Codner time to repair the damage.

In eight weeks the men dug about 12 metres. They were still 18 metres from the fence. It seemed an impossible target given the slow pace and the sweltering conditions. As the tunnel grew longer, sand had to be lugged a greater distance — a back-breaking chore in the musty, cramped space.

Then Williams became ill. For almost a week he was confined to the camp hospital, slowing down progress. He made good use of his time in bed, though. He chatted to other patients and pumped them for news about the war, the routes open and those blocked — information that might be of help when the men finally escaped.

While Williams, Codner and Philpot toiled in the tunnel, the escape committee also kept busy. The men would need civilian clothes once they left the camp. Tailors stitched clothing for the men from bedsheets, curtains, blankets, old uniforms and underwear — whatever was on hand. They also needed cover stories, new identities, passports, travel permits and other documents to get across occupied Europe. To create false papers, POWs skilled at forgery worked in secret, knowing that their talents spelled the difference between success and failure.

On October 29, 1943, nearly four months after the digging had started, the tunnel was almost finished. That afternoon when the vaulters carried the horse to its familiar spot, Williams and Codner were inside, their backs pressed against the ends of the horse, their feet propped on either side of the frame.

**The vaulting box made for an ingenious distraction
from the work happening underground.**

When the exercise period was over, prisoners carried back the horse. This time only Williams was inside. Codner stayed in the tunnel to dig the final section. With little air circulation at the end of the tunnel it was hard to breathe. Using a length of metal pipe, he rammed small holes into the tunnel roof, drawing in badly needed oxygen. By candlelight, he chipped at the dirt, centimetres closer to freedom with every scoop.

In the camp, Williams and Philpot gathered food, documents, money, clothing and travel papers that the escape committee had prepared. Around 4:00 p.m. the vaulters carried the horse out again. Kit bags containing supplies dangled from hooks inside, and this time three men were aboard: Williams, Philpot and a third prisoner. Philpot and Williams joined Codner in the tunnel. The other prisoner covered the tunnel entrance and then rode back when the vaulting horse was returned to the barracks.

At the far end of the tunnel, the three POWs changed into civilian clothes and distributed the supplies. They reviewed their cover stories, the escape routes they would follow and the things they would need to do or say along the way.

At 6:00 p.m., right on schedule, Williams and Codner broke through the remaining dirt. They climbed out of the tunnel just outside the prison fence. Philpot followed. Lively music and singing drifted from the barracks — a diversion planned by the escape committee to distract the German guards. They didn't notice the three men as they slipped into the thick woods outside the camp.

Soon after, the three men split up. Philpot, who was fluent in French and preferred to travel alone, headed toward neutral, war-free Sweden disguised as a French labourer. Williams and Codner, also disguised as French labourers, travelled together.

Dodging sniffer dogs and the German secret police, they hopped trains and ships until they reached the Swedish city of Göteborg. To their surprise, Philpot was already there, having beaten them by a full week. After contacting the British consul, the three flew back to England.

Heroes with stories to tell, Eric Williams wrote *The Wooden Horse*, a novel based on the escape, while Oliver Philpot wrote *Stolen Journey*, an account of his wartime adventures. For Richard Codner, the experience was a highlight, more exciting than dangerous. "I enjoyed myself when we were escaping," he once said. "There was something about it. We were really living then . . . I liked being hunted . . . the feeling that every minute was important, that everything you did would sway the balance."

CHISELLING OFF "THE ROCK"

One night four prisoners held at Alcatraz made a bid for freedom.

On a clear day, from the rocky island of Alcatraz where America's most famous prison stands, you can see the city of San Francisco. San Francisco Bay separates the prison from the city, and although the two are only 2.5 kilometres apart, danger lurks in the choppy waters between. Tides rule the bay, deep currents run strong and no less than eleven species of shark prowl the region. The water is bone-numbingly cold and frequent storms lash the coast.

From 1934 to 1961, in Alcatraz's first twenty-seven years as a federal prison, twenty-nine men tried to escape in twelve separate attempts. All failed. Some were caught long before reaching the water. Others made it off the island, only to be recaptured soon after. Two vanished — presumed drowned, their bodies swept out to sea.

With that kind of record, Alcatraz was thought to be escape-proof. Once on The Rock, there was no way for a prisoner to get off — at least not alive or until his sentence had been served.

The watchtowers at Alcatraz were just one of the ways to keep prisoners from escaping.

Despite the unlikelihood of escape, four prisoners at Alcatraz dreamed and schemed, anxious to shorten their stay. While those who break the law deserve justice, not admiration, these criminals are legendary for their carefully plotted plan.

The ringleader was Frank Morris, a career criminal with a long list of offences ranging from drug possession to armed robbery. The others — Allen West and brothers Clarence and John Anglin — were also ambitious criminals, sent to Alcatraz for robbing banks and hijacking cars.

In Alcatraz, the four men found one another in Cell Block B. They were confined to four separate cells. Morris and West were beside each other; the Anglin brothers in adjoining cells farther down the corridor. Cramped and windowless, the cells were just 1.5 metres by 2.7 metres, with a toilet and small sink on the far wall opposite the door, and a simple cot on another.

Outside, 3-metre-high walls topped with a fence and barbed wire ringed the prison. The walls were watched around the clock by armed guards. At night searchlights raked the courtyard. Inside, guards patrolled the corridors, peering into cells, counting heads and calling names, expecting prisoners to respond and prove they were still there.

A chance discovery gave the men an idea.

For a long while, the four prisoners plotted and planned. Escape seemed impossible. Then in September 1961 a chance discovery gave them an idea.

An unguarded utility corridor ran behind the solid wall of each cell. It was narrow — just 0.9 metres wide — and crammed with electrical cables, plumbing pipes and ventilation shafts that ran to the roof. The men noticed that the concrete around the air vents in the far wall of their cells had deteriorated. It crumbled easily, flaking off in small chunks with just a bit of scraping. And so an idea was born — freedom lay just behind the vent, down the utility corridor and up to the roof, if only they could break through.

Each evening after returning from work details, the four men chiselled at the concrete. They worked in pairs from adjoining cells, one being the lookout while the other attacked the concrete. To drown out the sound, they dug mostly during music hour when the squawk of accordions flooded the prison.

Their tools were simple — metal spoons stolen from the kitchen, drill bits from the workshop and equipment around the prison that no one would miss. When the prison's vacuum system broke down, Allen West dismantled it, removed the electric motor and made a drill to speed up the chiselling.

To avoid detection, the men stuck false panels painted to look like the original grill work over the vent openings. By draping a towel over the sink or dangling a pair of pants off a faucet, they hid the chipped concrete and its false panel.

It was one thing to break out of the cell. It was another to make it off the island. An article in a *Popular Mechanics* magazine spawned a solution to the problem. Using a method outlined in the article, the men built a raft from 50 green, prison-issued raincoats cut and glued together. Frank Morris modified an accordion-like instrument called a concertina and made a pump to inflate the vessel. West carved oars from plywood smuggled out of the maintenance shed. He also made inflatable life vests from raincoats, one for each of them.

To fool the guards, who made nightly head counts, the Anglin brothers crafted dummy heads out of soap and toilet paper. Topped with hair clippings swept off the barbershop floor and coated with flesh-tone paint stolen from prison art kits, the heads looked realistic enough to pass inspection.

After nine months each man had cut through the wall of his cell, providing access to the utility corridor. The blades and motor of a fan inside a ventilation shaft had been removed, opening a passage to the roof. The life vests, dummy heads, raft and oars waited, hidden on the roof above the utility corridor.

After lights-out on June 11, 1962, Morris squeezed through the ventilation hole and retrieved a dummy head. The Anglin brothers did the same. They tucked the heads under blankets fluffed with clothes to resemble bodies and then re-entered the corridor. The three men waited for West. The prison ran a tight schedule and time was everything that night. Where was he?

West had encountered a problem. Days before, his false grill had begun to slip. To hold the grill in place, he had used cement. The cement had set. While the others waited, he frantically chipped at the wall, but the grill stayed fixed in place. Escape was now impossible.

The others waited in the corridor as long as they dared. Finally they abandoned West. In the dark, the three climbed plumbing pipes to reach a small landing. They squeezed through a ventilation shaft that led to the roof and scrambled across 30 metres of rooftop. One by one they slithered down a vertical pipe that ran along the wall to the ground. Lugging the raft and life vests, the three skirted past water tanks, wound down a hill to the east side of the rocky island and headed to the water's edge.

The next morning a guard noticed something peculiar. One of the inmates refused to stir. Alarmed, the guard summoned Bill Long, the supervisor. Long stormed down the corridor to the prisoner's cell. It was a moment he never forgot.

"I reached my left hand through the bars and hit the pillow and hollered 'Get up for count!'" he told a reporter years later. "*Bam*, the head flopped off on the floor. They said I jumped back four feet from the bars."

The prison supervisor sounded the alarm, setting off a desperate manhunt. From prison rooftop to rocky shore, guards searched every corner of the island. Boats scoured the bay and San Francisco police watched streets and highways, looking for signs of the prisoners or the route they might have taken.

Neither the escaped prisoners nor their bodies were ever found. The only tangible evidence discovered was the chiselled openings in the cells, the dummy heads hidden in the beds, a wooden paddle recovered from a nearby island and three vests found in various places — one in the bay, one in the ocean and another on the prison roof.

Afterward, Alcatraz was never quite the same. Loopholes

in security were tightened to prevent such escapes in the future. And while Alcatraz the prison is no longer operational, Alcatraz the tourist attraction is. On guided tours, visitors to The Rock peer into the cells of the four infamous prisoners, intrigued by the complexity of their escape.

Did the inmates make it or die trying? The FBI file is still open and active, pending further information.

THE BROTHERS THREE

Ingo Bethke missed his two brothers. And that led to even more clever and dangerous escapes.

Darkness shrouded the Elbe River. For twenty-one-year-old Ingo Bethke, the river was like an old friend beckoning him. For months he had studied the Elbe. He knew the river's twists and turns, the positions of watchtowers along its east bank, the places that were guarded and those that were not. He'd come this far. There would be no turning back.

The Elbe snaked across northern Germany, part of the highly protected border that from 1961 to 1990 cut across the country, preventing citizens in communist East Germany from crossing into democratically run West Germany. The Inner German Border, a 1381-kilometre-long system of protective fences, barbed wire and watchtowers, separated the two countries. The Berlin Wall added another 155 kilometres of heavily guarded border. Many East Germans attempted to escape to West Germany across one of these barriers. Some succeeded. Many were captured. Others died, shot down while trying.

Workers embed pieces of broken glass atop the Berlin Wall
to keep East Berliners from escaping.

That night in May 1975, Ingo stood on the bank of the
Elbe in East Germany. He gazed at lights glimmering in West
Germany only 150 metres away. A friend stood beside him,
another young man who had heard the call of freedom and
was prepared to risk everything.

The two had rented a car and driven 80 kilometres north
of East Berlin to this remote and isolated place along the
river. A metal fence ran alongside the Elbe there. It was
topped with razor wire, protected by land mines and rigged
with trip wires that activated floodlights and alerted armed
guards. After months of studying this place, Ingo decided it
was where their chances would be best.

Taking advantage of the dark, the two men abandoned the

car. They tiptoed across a strip of sand planted with mines, sneaked through the fence — careful not to trigger alarms — and crept down to the water's edge.

The Elbe was the last obstacle in their way, the point of no return in their plan. The two friends blew up air mattresses they carried. They slid them into the Elbe and climbed aboard. Paddling in silence, they crossed the river, leaving families and possessions behind to begin new lives on the West German side.

As a hunted man, Ingo knew that he could never return to East Germany, and while freedom brought him better jobs and greater opportunities, it came with a price. He missed his two younger brothers, Holger and Egbert. As it turned out, his brothers missed him, too. And that led to escapes even more clever and dangerous.

* * *

For eight years Ingo and his brothers kept in touch with secret phone calls and coded messages. With him gone, life grew more complicated for Holger and Egbert. They were questioned by the East German police and followed everywhere. Privileges were withdrawn; any chance for better jobs or higher pay quashed. Over time, security was tightened all along the border, especially along the Berlin Wall, where guards patrolled day and night, armed and ready.

In 1983 Michael Becker, a friend of Holger's who had similar dreams of escape, spotted an article in a smuggled West German magazine that described daring escapes over the Berlin Wall. One captured his attention — a family who had used cables, pulleys and a harness to slide to the West German side.

Michael shared his idea with Holger. "I told him I had a plan with an eighty per cent chance of working. His eyes lit up and he said: 'Count me in. I'm with you.'"

To start, Michael ordered wooden rollers from a carpentry shop. They were 15 centimetres in diameter, 2.5 centimetres thick and had a deep groove running down the middle. Then he obtained 90 metres of steel cable from a friend who worked at a crane-making factory.

Holger and Michael rented a car and drove along part of the Berlin Wall which separated East and West Berlin, looking for a proper site. At the intersection of two streets, Holger spotted a five-storey housing complex that faced a row of four-storey apartment buildings in West Berlin.

"We inspected the inside of the house," Michael said. "Dressed in overalls as repairmen, we went up to the attic — which Holger opened with a skeleton key — made sketches, checked to see that the chimney was big and solid and that the little skylight windows on the roof were big enough for us. It was all perfect."

Next they looked for a place to practise. In a public park on the edge of the city, they attached one end of the steel cable to a tree about 7 metres above ground, wrapped it around another tree at a height of 5 metres and then secured the tail end to the bumper of their car. For two weeks the pair ran drills in broad daylight. Pulled by gravity, they scooted down the zip line, riding the cable by hanging on to the wooden rollers. When people asked questions, they answered, "We're training for the circus."

They found a bow and arrow, a key piece of equipment for their plan. They set up targets in a meadow near Soviet head-quarters, where Holger shot arrow after arrow, gaining confidence and accuracy.

To make the plan work, they needed someone on the West Berlin side. Holger sent Ingo letters with fake return addresses. Will you help? he asked. Ingo agreed. They set a date for their escape — March 30, Holger's birthday.

That afternoon Holger said goodbye to Egbert, the only other person besides his older brother who knew of their plan. Pretending to be electricians, Holger and Michael snuck into the apartment block in East Berlin. Lugging wires, cables, fishing line, a walkie-talkie, blankets, sandwiches, the bow and four arrows, and an electrician's tool kit, they trudged up five flights of stairs to the attic. To reduce noise they padded their shoes with foam.

"We're training for the circus."

They waited. The sun dipped over the horizon, stars appeared and coolness settled over the city. One by one, nearby apartments fell silent. At 3:00 a.m. they switched on the walkie-talkie. A familiar voice crackled over the airway. *"Ich bin hier* — I'm here. Are you ready?" It was Ingo, positioned in the building on the other side of the Berlin Wall.

Holger attached fishing line to an arrow, leaned out the skylight window and with directions provided by Ingo over the walkie-talkie, took aim at the West Berlin apartment. The first shot ran wild and landed in a tree. The second ended up on the roof of another building, fishing line trailing after it. A third arrow spiralled into a courtyard behind. While Ingo searched for it, Holger clung to the only arrow left — his last chance at freedom if Ingo failed to find the other arrow.

After an hour and a half of searching, Ingo spotted the arrow in a tall bush. He reeled in the fishing line, then a thicker cord attached to it and finally the steel cable. Holger tied his end around the brick chimney. Ingo secured his to the balcony of the apartment, and the rest to his car. To pull the cable tight, he drove forward.

Holger tied a rope around his waist and fastened it to the wooden roller. After making sure that a guard in a nearby watchtower was distracted, Holger zipped down the cable, soaring 20 metres above the street and over the Berlin Wall to Ingo, who was waiting on the balcony of the apartment on other side. It took a mere ten seconds. After unhooking himself, Holger called Michael over.

Reunited in West Berlin, the brothers hugged and rejoiced. Their joy, though, was tempered with regret. Egbert was still trapped in East Berlin.

* * *

With his two brothers gone, Egbert was followed closely by East German police. They tapped his phone, intercepted his mail and grilled friends and neighbours with questions. Once they offered him a free ticket to the West. It was a trap, a test of Egbert's loyalty, and Egbert knew it. He turned down the offer. "I like East Germany and I'm staying," he told them. Meanwhile his dream of escape grew.

In Cologne, West Germany, Ingo and Holger bought a bar and settled into life as business partners. Egbert was in their thoughts, though. How could they get their brother over the border?

One day in 1985, while attending a fair, Ingo and Holger bumped into two French pilots who told them about a tiny two-person aircraft called an ultralight. Fascinated, the brothers travelled to France to try one. The plane was flimsy and simple — 10-metre-long wings attached to a superlight, 2-metre metal frame; an open cockpit with two seats side by side; a small engine for power; two tiny wheels for takeoff and landing. Made for easy transport, the whole plane could be dismantled, packed into a trailer, hauled to a new location and reassembled.

"This is it," Ingo told Holger.

An ultralight aircraft might be the brothers' only hope
of bringing Egbert home.

The brothers sold their bar and bought two ultralights with
the money. Ingo took flying lessons. Afterward he taught Holger what he knew. They practised, assembling their machines,
taking them apart and flying whenever they could. They would
have only one chance. Success, and the lives of all three, depended on skill and perfect timing.

In May 1989, after four years of preparation, Ingo and Holger
drove to West Berlin. They sent a coded message to Egbert: *Ulricke
is doing well.* Egbert knew the meaning: *Be ready. We're coming.*

At midnight on May 25 the wind was soft, the sky clear. In
a park in West Berlin, Ingo and Holger unloaded their ultralights and assembled the pieces. To confuse border guards,
they had painted a Soviet star on the tail of each plane.

After checking wires and gauges, they donned flight suits and
helmets equipped with radios. Meanwhile, 6 kilometres away

in East Berlin, Egbert crept behind bushes in Treptower Park, a stone's throw from the Berlin Wall, a radio transmitter in his hand.

Just after 4:00 a.m. Ingo and Holger started their engines and rolled into position. In minutes they were aloft and zooming over the Berlin Wall. Soon Treptower Park soared into view.

"Are you there?" Ingo said over his radio.

"Yes, I am," Egbert radioed back.

Holger circled above, ready to help if problems arose while Ingo descended to scoop up Egbert. The moment the plane touched down, Egbert ran from the bushes and jumped into the empty seat. Ingo handed his brother a helmet, flashed a smile of welcome and gunned the engine.

With an extra person on board, liftoff was slow, but finally they cleared the trees that ringed the park. Eleven minutes and two seconds from the start of the operation, the two planes were back in West Berlin, three brothers free and reunited.

"I thought I'd never see my brothers again," Egbert said. "But they came out of the sky like angels and took me to paradise."

OUTSMARTING THE IMPOSSIBLE
October, 1964 / Berlin, Germany

In April 1964, under the leadership of Wolfgang Fuchs, a twenty-five-year-old optician, thirty students from the Free University of Berlin began digging a tunnel under the Berlin Wall. Their goal was simple — construct an escape route for students, friends and family members who were trapped in East Berlin.

While lookouts kept watch from surrounding rooftops, the students wielded shovels and pickaxes.

They started in an abandoned West Berlin bakery at 97 Bernauer Street. Progress was slow but steady. Six months later they broke through to the other side — the courtyard of an unused building in East Berlin.

The first night twenty-nine people, at ten-minute intervals, squeezed through the 90-centimetre-high tunnel, crawling on their hands and knees for 145 metres. The next night, twenty-eight more escaped.

"The marks of their knee prints in the tunnel floor looked like the ripples on a beach left behind by the receding tide," Fuchs said. "I will never forget that. That is beautiful."

Unfortunately, the tunnel was discovered by East Berlin police shortly after, rendering other escapes impossible. Nevertheless, fifty-seven refugees — including ten children — crawled through what became known as Tunnel 57, the longest and deepest tunnel ever constructed under the Berlin Wall.

NOW OR NEVER

Only a fence stood between Shin In Geun and freedom.

The snow was heavy and deep on the mountain slope where Shin In Geun stood. The air was crisp; the sun bright in the cloudless sky. A cold January wind blew across the forest, but otherwise conditions were perfect for the work he and other prisoners had been assigned — trimming trees and stacking firewood on the northern edge of Camp 14, a political prison in North Korea.

From his place on the slope, Shin watched the guard tower

400 metres away. It marked the outer limits of a 3-metre-high electrified fence that ran around the camp. Guards armed with automatic weapons patrolled the perimeter, halting any attempts to escape.

No one had ever escaped Camp 14. A number tried, but none succeeded. In the camp, prisoners had been brainwashed to spy on each other. Torture and execution awaited those who failed to inform on their neighbours. Those who dreamed of escape were caught long before they reached the fence.

But Shin had a plan, and that day on the mountain, escape beckoned him. Timing was everything. It was now or never.

* * *

Camp 14 lies in the middle of North Korea. It cuts a swath about 48 kilometres long and 24 kilometres wide along a steep mountain valley. Around fifteen thousand people live at Camp 14. No one knows the exact number because North Korea is a military-run country ruled by a dictator. Information is heavily guarded and controlled.

North Korean soldiers march past Kim Il Sung Square during a mass military parade.

In North Korea, citizens have few rights. Those who oppose the government often disappear. Many end up in slave-labour camps, places like Camp 14 where they toil for the rest of their lives at back-breaking tasks, never to taste freedom.

Shin In Geun knew no other life than Camp 14. He had been born and raised there, the child of parents who were political prisoners. The guards were his keepers and teachers, and almost daily Shin received stern lectures. His parents had sinned against the government, Shin was told, and he had to pay for their sins.

That meant hard labour at farms, in mines and in factories that dotted Camp 14 — places where the sun rarely shone and beatings and torture were common. Those in Camp 14 were encouraged to inform on fellow prisoners to earn special rewards — an extra glob of porridge or a fleeting moment of trust from the guards.

Shin's body told his tale of abuse. At twenty-three years old, he was short and slight, stunted from malnutrition; he weighed less than 54 kilograms. Food was scarce in Camp 14 — a few kernels of corn supplemented by rats Shin caught, cooked and ate. From years of heavy lifting, his arms were bowed. The middle finger on his right hand was partly missing, hacked off as punishment after Shin dropped a heavy sewing machine.

Shin's back, buttocks and legs were covered with ropey scars and discoloured patches. When he was thirteen years old, his mother and older brother had attempted to escape. Shin overhead their whispered plans. He knew the often re-peated rule of Camp 14: *Any witness to an attempted escape who fails to report it will be shot immediately.*

Obeying the camp rule, Shin told a night guard what he knew.

The next morning Shin was handcuffed, blindfolded and taken to an underground cell. "Your mother and brother were caught trying to escape," he was told. "Were you aware of this fact? If you want to live, you should spit out the truth."

Shin protested, explaining that he had informed a guard the night before. No one believed him. The night guard had apparently passed on the information, but had not given Shin credit for bringing it to his attention.

For days Shin was interrogated and tortured. Trussed with ropes, he was hung by his arms and legs from the ceiling, his body slung in a U with his bare back to the floor. A tub of burning charcoal was shoved beneath him. Shin was lowered. To hold him in place, the guards pierced his abdomen with a hook. The pain was excruciating.

Anger simmered inside him for the torture he had been forced to endure.

Eventually Shin passed out. He awoke in a cell, his back blistered and his ankles raw from the shackles that bound him. Months later, after his wounds had healed and guards had abandoned their questioning, he and his father were driven, handcuffed and blindfolded, to a site where they were forced to witness the execution of Shin's mother and brother. Anger simmered inside Shin — anger at his father for the life he was forced to lead; anger at his mother and brother for the torture he had been forced to endure.

In March 2003 Shin was transferred to the camp's garment factory. When sewing machines broke down, he fixed them.

Then in October he was given another assignment. He was introduced to a new prisoner, Park Yong Chul. "Park needs to confess," the factory superintendent told Shin.

Under the guise of showing Park how to fix sewing machines, Shin befriended him, hoping to find out about his past, his politics, his family — information that he could feed back to the superintendent who had promised Shin rewards in return. Park spoke openly. A well-educated and travelled man, he told Shin about life outside Camp 14. He talked about the wonders of technology — cars, computers, televisions, mobile phones. He shared lessons in geography. A place called China neighboured North Korea; South Korea and Japan were not far off either. People there were rich, Park said. They had jobs, money, food.

Shin savoured Park's descriptions of steaming dishes and luscious desserts. In Camp 14 he was always hungry. He could scarcely imagine a world where plates were full and stomachs were never empty.

Although Shin was supposed to tell the factory superintendent what he knew, he kept the information secret. He dreamed of a different future. He imagined life beyond the prison fence. He thought about breaking free.

Shin told Park about his dream of freedom. It was a risky move. What if Park was an informer, planted in the sewing factory to spy on him? But Shin's dream was stronger than his fear. To escape, he needed Park. Park knew the way to China. Park had connections outside Camp 14 — relatives and friends who would help them along the way.

Together the two men plotted their escape. From his days of gathering wood on the mountain slope, Shin knew about the electrified fence. To escape they would have to get near the fence, dodge guards who kept an armed watch, then find some way to climb over or squeeze through the fence without touching the electrified wires.

Shin and Park waited for an excuse to get close to the fence. In late December 2004 Shin learned that the factory was scheduled to close for two days in January. He, Park and other factory workers would be assigned other jobs — trimming trees and stacking wood on a mountain ridge on the eastern edge of the camp.

Opportunity called. Now or never, it seemed to say.

* * *

Early on the morning of January 2, 2005, Shin, Park and twenty-five other prisoners plodded around the snowy slope. Between swings of his axe, Shin watched the guards who patrolled the inside perimeter of the electrified fence. He observed their patterns. The guards walked in pairs. They carried automatic weapons. Between shifts there were lengthy gaps, times when guards were elsewhere.

Shin and Park waited until dusk, since darkness offered protection. Once they got over the fence, it would be difficult for guards to follow their footprints in the snow as they led down the steep slope, through forests and past rocky outcroppings.

At four o'clock the two edged close to the fence, trimming trees as they moved. They watched the guards and waited for a lull in coverage. No one seemed to notice them.

Park hesitated. "Can we try it some other time?"

The time was now, Shin felt. They might never have another chance. He grabbed Park's hand. "Let's run," he said.

Partway to the fence, Shin slipped on the ice and fell. Park ran ahead. Strands of high-voltage barbed wire spaced about 30 centimetres apart and strung between tall poles stood between him and freedom. As long as he didn't touch the wires, he'd pass through unharmed.

Park didn't wait for Shin. He shoved his arms, head and shoulders between the lowest two strands of wire. Shin saw sparks and smelled the stench of burning flesh. Park twitched, then stopped moving. His body sagged on the wire, pulling it down, creating a small gap between the strands.

The fence had claimed his friend; it could just as easily kill him.

There wasn't anything Shin could do for Park. In that instant he felt his plan dissolve. Park knew the way to China. Park spoke the languages Shin needed. Park had connections in different countries. Without Park, what chance did he have? The fence had claimed his friend; it could just as easily kill him. The guards would be returning soon. It was now or never. Shin had only seconds to decide.

Without looking back, he crawled over Park, hoping that his friend's body would protect him from the electrified fence. Even with Park shielding him, Shin felt a surge of electricity along the soles of his feet. When he was almost through the gap, his lower legs slipped off Park and struck the bottom wire. A jolt of electricity shot through his body. "I almost fainted," Shin said.

The smell of burning flesh was strong now — his or Park's, Shin couldn't tell. He pushed on, squirmed over Park and slid through the gap. For a few moments excitement replaced pain and fear. "I was overwhelmed by joy. The feeling of ecstasy to be out of the camp was beyond description."

Shin barrelled down the slope, through heavy snow, past stands of trees. No shots followed him, no shouts of alarm. For two hours he ran, fuelled by adrenaline and drawn by freedom, going the only direction that seemed reasonable — downhill. When he reached a valley, Shin stopped. He felt something sticky trickling down his leg. He rolled up his pants. Blood oozed from wounds along his legs, damage caused by the jolt of electricity when he passed over Park.

For two hours he ran, fuelled by adrenaline and drawn by freedom.

Without Park to guide him, Shin had no idea where to go. He relied on instinct and deception, skills he had acquired at Camp 14. He broke into a farmer's shed and stole a military uniform. Wearing it, he was no longer a runaway prisoner, just another poorly clothed, undernourished North Korean soldier. As he travelled through towns, he ate scraps stolen from gardens or garbage bins. He slept wherever he could find shelter — in pigpens, haystacks, freight cars. He bartered and bargained and bribed. He exploited the goodness of others and found jobs, staying just long enough to earn money before moving on.

Although Shin was cold, hungry, in pain and still in North Korea, he felt strangely renewed. This is what freedom is like, he told himself. Life was whatever he wanted to make of it now.

Eventually Shin reached the Tumen River. On the other side lay China. Pretending to be a soldier, he bribed border guards with crackers, cigarettes and bags of sweets. Here the river was shallow and frozen, about 90 metres wide. Given the go-ahead by the guard, Shin walked across the fragile ice. Halfway to China the ice broke. Wet and cold, Shin crawled the rest of the way.

China was just the beginning for Shin. Within two years he was in South Korea, where he wrote *Escape to the Outside World*, his memoir about life in Camp 14. Two years later he was in southern California, adjusting to new languages and western ways. American journalist Blaine Harden picked up Shin's story and wrote another account titled *Escape from Camp 14*.

Although his transition to a new life has not been easy, Shin is motivated by purpose. "If the world knows about the camp and if this improves the situation of people inside, this is the least I can do to repay the fellow prisoners who saved my life, kept me alive and helped me escape."

EPILOGUE

This book is about people who faced danger, risk and impossible situations. Somehow they overcame enormous obstacles, conquering death, injury, imprisonment and even torture to emerge triumphant. How did they survive the impossible?

For many, the answer lies in the creative ways they tackled problems. The expression "thinking outside the box" is often used to describe situations like these, where clever thinking pierces a barrier that seems impenetrable, allowing a groundbreaking solution to seep through.

For some in this book, thinking outside the box took on an inventive form. When Chilean miners became trapped underground, for example, rescuers tackled the problem by creating new devices — miniature cameras to peer below, *paloma* to shuttle supplies, the Phoenix to bring the men to the surface. Others tinkered with objects and spaces, modifying them to serve a new purpose, such as the Houston engineers on the Apollo 13 mission.

For Saroo Munshi Khan and Asmaa Mahfouz, out-of-the-box thinking meant something else. Saroo put a fresh spin on Google Earth and used it unlike anyone had before. Asmaa channelled YouTube's popularity and used it as a rallying cry for political change in Egypt. Taking something ordinary and using it in an unconventional way is one method of overcoming obstacles.

William Kamkwamba demonstrated another, borrowing an idea from a science book, adjusting it to suit his own situation. Borrowing an idea helped rescuers in Peru to save 72 hostages, too.

For people like Henry "Box" Brown, the source of inspiration is more mysterious. Brown wrote that "the idea just flashed into my mind." In some situations, solutions seem to leap out of thin air without will or effort.

Experience and knowledge counted immensely in some cases. Both of Juliane Koepcke's parents were zoologists, and she knew the jungle better than most — enough to follow a stream to civilization, enough to recognize the call of a hoatzin and know that she was near open water. Pilot Chesley Sullenberger, with thousands of hours of flight time to his credit, knew that the Hudson River was his only option. In these and other cases, experience tipped the scales, giving people choices not available to others. The wonder is that with danger clawing at their thoughts, they were able to stifle panic and recall what they knew in order to use it so effectively.

Thinking outside the box took different forms in this book, and words like invent, modify, adapt, create and insight have been used to describe its many shades. But inventive thinking doesn't explain everything. To conquer the impossible, it takes more than just a clever solution. It takes strength of character, too. Qualities like Eric Le Marque's never-give-up attitude, Corrie ten Boom's courage, the Chilean miners' all-for-one spirit. Determination, persistence, compassion, cooperation, optimism — these and other qualities kept hope alive and the goal firmly in sight. When creative solutions did appear, they flourished, anchored in fertile soil and nurtured by do-or-die attitudes.

Perhaps that is a lesson we can draw from such stories. In times of trouble, when the impossible rears its ugly head and all seems lost, qualities that reside inside us — those characteristics that define who we are and make us strong — can count as much as, and sometimes even more than, the out-of-the-box solutions we might create.

ACKNOWLEDGEMENTS

Fearless people populate this book. From each story I drew inspiration, awed by the boldness and strength of their actions. Without these individuals' daring and often creative responses to a challenge, there would be no book to write. First and foremost in my list of gratitudes, I offer them my thanks.

To bring any book to completion takes teamwork, and this book is no exception. I am indebted to a number of dedicated individuals affiliated with Scholastic Canada who stood behind this book, generously lending their talents to shape its final form. My sincerest thanks to Senior Editor Sandy Bogart Johnston, who cultivated the idea, sharpened its focus and fine-tuned the content. Thanks as well to Carrie Gleason for skilfully editing the manuscript, bringing fresh perspectives to the material and asking that all important question: Why? I am also grateful to others on the Scholastic team who contributed to this venture, in particular Publisher Diane Kerner and Art Director Aldo Fierro.

Lastly, thank you to family, friends, fellow writers and ardent readers who, in ways large and small, encourage and inspire. A special nod to my home team and especially my wife, Jo, who cheers me on daily, steering me past obstacles and over hurdles — my deepest thanks.

FOR FURTHER READING

Franklin, Jonathan. (2011). *The 33: The Ultimate Account of the Chilean Miners' Dramatic Rescue.* Transworld Publishers Limited.

Goldfield, David J. (2007). *The Ambassador's Word: Hostage Crisis in Peru, 1996-1997.* Penumbra Press.

Harden, Blaine. (2012). *Escape from Camp 14: One man's remarkable odyssey from North Korea to freedom in the West.* Viking.

Kamkwamba, William. (2009). *The Boy Who Harnessed the Wind: Creating Currents of Electricity & Hope.* William Morrow.

Koepcke, Juliane. (2011). *When I Fell From the Sky.* Titletown Publishing.

Lovell, James & Kluger, Jeffrey. (1994). *Lost Moon: The Perilous Voyage of Apollo 13.* Houghton Mifflin.

O'Shei, Tim. (2007). *Stranded in the Snow! Eric LeMarque's Story of Survival.* Capstone Press.

Philpot, Oliver. (1952). *Stolen Journey.* Dutton.

Sullenberger, Chesley. (2009). *Highest Duty: My Search For What Really Matters.* William Morrow.

ten Boom, Corrie with Elizabeth & John Sherrill. (1984). *The Hiding Place.* Bantam Books, Reprint Edition

Williams, Eric. (1985, revised). *The Wooden Horse.* Penguin.

IMAGE CREDITS